SATAN UNMASKED & MYSTERY BABYLON

Gerald B. Shugart

Lulu Publishing | Morrisville, North Carolina

SATAN UNMASKED & MYSTERY BABYLON

by

Gerald B. Shugart

Copyright, ©2021 by Gerald B. Shugart

FIRST EDITION

ISBN: 978-BOWKER-ISBN

All rights reserved. No part of this book may be reproduced in any form without permission in writing, except in the case of brief quotations in specific Bible studies, critical articles or reviews.

All quoted sources and Bible translations are the property of their respective owners.

Formatting conducted by ShelfBloom ePress. Concerns about formatting, typographical errors, etc. should be sent to support@shelfbloom.com

DEDICATION

In Loving Memory of my Mother, Lorena Brown Shugart, and of my Father, Jack Alton Shugart, and of my Sister, Jane Shugart Pontigo.

Table of Contents

Chapter I | The Devil Made Me Do It   1

Chapter II | Religion from Ancient Times   5

Chapter III | The Witness of the Stars   9

Chapter IV | The Perversion of the Zodiac   18

Chapter V | Mystery, Babylon the Great   29

Chapter VI | Satan Blinds the Eyes of Unbelievers   48

Chapter VII | The Rite of Water Baptism   62

Chapter VIII | Infant Baptism and Original Sin   82

Chapter IX | The Popes and Priests of Rome   115

Chapter X | The Sacrifice of the Mass   136

Chapter XI | Mary as Portrayed by Rome   149

Chapter XII | Conclusion   163

Appendices | 1-7   178

Satan Unmasked & Mystery Babylon

The Battle Lines Are Drawn

Introduction

The Apostle Paul likens the Christian's struggle with Satan to a battle where they are to put on the "whole armour of God":

"Finally, my brethren, be strong in the Lord, and in the power of his might. Put on the whole armour of God, that ye may be able to stand against the wiles of the devil. For we wrestle not against flesh and blood, but against principalities, against powers, against the rulers of the darkness of this world, against spiritual wickedness in high places. Wherefore take unto you the whole armour of God, that ye may be able to withstand in the evil day, and having done all, to stand. Stand therefore, having your loins girt about with truth, and having on the breastplate of righteousness; And your feet shod with the preparation of the gospel of peace; Above all, taking the shield of faith, wherewith ye shall be able to quench all the fiery darts of the wicked. And take the helmet of salvation, and the sword of the Spirit, which is the word of God" (Eph. 6:10-17). [1]

Today there is much confusion concerning Satan and his methods. For instance, Clarance Larkin wrote, *"There are many who deny the existence of Satan. They claim that what we call Satan is only a 'principle of evil.' That this 'evil' is a sort of 'malaria,' an intangible thing like disease germs that floats about in the atmosphere and attacks people's hearts under certain conditions."* [2]

There are many Christians who assert that the following prophecy has already been fulfilled:

"*And I saw an angel come down from heaven, having the key of the bottomless pit and a great chain in his hand. And he laid hold on the dragon, that old serpent, which is the Devil, and Satan, and bound him a thousand years*" (Rev.20:1-2).

James B. Richards wrote, "*Who is Satan, really? Far too many Christians have a distorted image of the devil. Contrary to popular belief, he is not a powerful spiritual being! He is a defeated foe; Jesus has stripped him of all power and authority.*" **3**

G.K. Beale wrote, "*The binding was probably inaugurated during Christ's ministry, which is more the focus of texts such as Matt. 12:29; Mark 3:27; and Luke 10:17-19. Satan's binding was climactically put in motion immediately after Christ's resurrection, and it lasts throughout most of the age between Christ's first and second comings.*" **4**

If Satan was bound after the Lord Jesus' resurrection then why did Peter write the following just a few years after the Lord Jesus' resurrection?:

"*Be sober, be vigilant; because your adversary the devil, as a roaring lion, walketh about, seeking whom he may devour*" (1 Pet.5:18).

It's unfortunate that Christians all over the world remain in a state of uncertainity concerning the methods and schemes of Satan:

"*For if the trumpet give an uncertain sound, who shall prepare himself to the battle?*" (1 Cor.14:8).

The following verse gives us a clue as to Satan's methods:

"*And the great dragon was cast out, that old serpent, called the Devil, and Satan, which deceiveth the whole world: he was cast out into the earth, and his angels were *cast out with him*" (Rev.12:9).

It is said that Satan "*deceiveth the whole world*" and in that role he is at the present time deceiving hundreds of million people about the gospel which saves:

"*The god of this world hath blinded the minds of them which believe not, lest the light of the glorious gospel of Christ, who is the image of God, should shine unto them*" (2 Cor.4:4).

The glorious gospel of Christ is the "gospel of the grace of God" (Acts 20:24) and that is the gospel which saves all those who believe it:

"*For I am not ashamed of the gospel of Christ: for it is the power of God unto salvation to every one that believeth*" (Ro.1:16).

The chapters of this book which follow will reveal exactly how Satan is blinding the minds of hundreds of millions of the unsaved to the light of the gospel of the grace of God.

End Notes

1. Unless otherwise noted, all Biblical passages referenced are from the King James Bible (KJV).

2. Clarence Larkin, *The Spirit World* (Rev.Clarence Larkin Estate, 1921), 8.

3. James B. Richards *Satan Unmasked: The Truth Behind The Lie* (Travelers Rest, SC: Milestone International Publishers, 2004), Quoted From Back Cover.

4. G. K. Beale, *The Book of Revelation* (Grand Rapids, MI: William B. Eerdmans Publishing Company. 1999), 985.

Chapter I. The Devil Made Me Do It

In the 1970s comedian Flip Wilson popularized the saying "The devil made me do it." On his television show Flip's character Geraldine Jones was always doing things which she knew would infuriate her husband, such as buying a very expensive dress. When confronted by her husband she said, "the devil made me buy this dress." Geraldine and her catch-phrase took the country by storm and when anyone was caught doing something naughty the excuse was always, "the devil made me do it." Unbelievers found it amusing but ludicrous but to many in Christendom that is exactly what they had been taught. After all, the idea that Satan tempts "all" people to evil is taught in the church at Rome, as witnessed by the words of Pope John Paul II when he said that "*the devil, the 'prince of this world,' even today continues his deceitful action. Every man, over and above his own concupiscence and the bad example of others, is also tempted by the devil, and the more so when he is least aware of it.*" [1]

Is Pope Paul II correct when he states that the insidious voice of Satan is heard by "every person"?:

"*In the inner heart of every person the voice of God and the insidious voice of the Evil One can be heard. The latter seeks to deceive the human person, seducing him with the prospect of false goods, to lead him away from the real good that consists precisely in fulfilling the divine will.*" [2]

Sir Robert Anderson wrote, "*if the majority of the many thousands of millions of mankind are thus under his personal influence, he must be acquainted with the life and circumstances of each individual. Are we, then, to conclude that he is practically omnipresent and omniscient? Are we to ascribe to him these attributes of Deity?*" [3]

According to Anderson, "*Men dream of a devil, horned and hoofed - a hideous and obscene monster - who haunts the squalid slums and gilded vice-dens of our cities, and tempts the depraved to acts of atrocity or shame. But, according to Holy Writ, he 'fashions himself into an angel of light,' and 'his ministers fashion themselves as ministers of righteousness' (2 Cor.xi 14). Do 'ministers of righteousness' corrupt men's morals or incite them to commit outrages?...No one may assert*" says Anderson, "*that Satan might not use the basest means to ensnare a minister of Christ, and thus mar his testimony and destroy his usefulness. But it cannot be asserted too often or too plainly that his normal effort is not to tempt to the commission of sins such as lead to contrition, and teach us how weak we are; but, by drawing us away to mere human morality, or religion, or philosophy, to deaden or destroy our sense of dependence upon God. For sin may humble a Christian; but human philosophy and religion can only foster his self-esteem. And pride is 'the snare of the devil ; not humility.*" [4]

The Deceiver of the Whole World

Anderson says that "*In his 'devices' upon men the Satan of Scripture is the enemy, not of morals, but of 'faith.'*" [5]

The believer is told to resist Satan by "standing firm in the faith":

"*Be alert and of sober mind. Your enemy the devil prowls around like a roaring lion looking for someone to devour. Resist him, standing firm in the faith*" (1Pet.5:8-9; NIV).

In the parable of the sower Satan takes the word of God out of the hearts of those who hear it lest that they should believe and be saved:

"*Those by the way side are they that hear; then cometh the devil, and taketh away the word out of their hearts, lest they should believe and be saved*" (Lk.8:12).

Satan Controls the Religions of This World

"*The god of this world*" is his awful title--a title Divinely conceded to the Evil One," Anderson writes of Satan, "*not because the Supreme has delegated His sovereignty, but because the world accords him its homage. It is in the sphere of religion, then, that the influence of the Tempter is to be sought - not in the records of our criminal courts, not in the pages of obscene novels, but in the teaching of false theologies...the Satan cult is to be sought for, not in pagan orgies, but in the acceptance of the Eden gospel, and the pursuit of religious systems, which honour man and dishonour Christ.*" [6]

Dave Hunt wrote that "*Religion was always the dominant element in ancient world empires...Priests, soothsayers, and sorcerers were the closest advisers to rulers for thousands of years, and in most instances were the real power behind the throne...Atheism is not Satan's major weapon in his campaign to deceive mankind into following him. He himself is not an atheist, for his great ambition, 'I will be like the Most High [i. e. God]' (Isaiah 14:14), itself acknowledges God's existence...As 'the god of this world,' Satan weapon is 'false religions and the deceitful promises they present,' which turn aside those who believe them from knowing God's truth.*" [7]

With this in mind let us now look at the most ancient religions and what was believed about God before the great flood, before God gave mankind a written revelation.

End Notes

1. Pope John Paul II, *ANGELUS*, 17 February 2002.

2. Pope John Paul II, *ANGELUS*, 9 March 2003.

3. Sir Robert Anderson, *The Silence of God* (Grand Rapids, MI: Kregel Publications, 1978), 190.

4. *Ibid,*, 126,195.

5. *Ibid.*, 184.

6. *Ibid.*, 127, 131

7. Dave Hunt, *A Woman Rides the Beast* (Eugene, OR: Harvest House Publishers, 1994), 43.

Chapter II. Religions From Ancient Times

The Trinity

Alexander Hislop wrote, "*The ancient Babylonians, just as the modern Romans, recognized in words the unity of the Godhead; and, while worshipping innumerable minor deities, as possessed of certain influence on human affairs, they distinctly acknowledged that there was ONE infinite and almighty Creator, supreme over all.*" [1]

According to Hislop, "*In the unity of that one Only God of the Babylonians, there were three persons...In Japan, the Buddhists worship their great divinity, Buddah, with three heads, in the very same form, under the name of 'San Pao Fuh.' All these have existed from ancient times. While overlaid with idolatry, the recognition of a Trinity was universal in all the ancient nations of the world, proving how deep-rooted in the human race was the primeval doctrine of this subject*" [2]

The word "primeval" means "of the earliest ages in the history of the world." So before the flood and before God gave His written word through Moses the belief in a Triune God existed in all the ancient nations of the world. How was that possible unless God did reveal that truth to mankind before He revealed His truths in writing? There can be no doubt that God did reveal the facts concerning the Trinity before the great flood.

The Babylonian Madonna and Son

Hilsop continues, writing that "*While this had been the original way in which Pagan idolatry had represented the Triune God...an important change had taken place in the Babylonian notions in regard to the divinity; and that the three persons had come to be, the Eternal Father, the Spirit of God incarnate in a human mother, and a Divine Son, the fruit of that incarnation....While this was the theory, the first person in the Godhead was practically overlooked. As the Great Invisible, taking no immediate concern in human affairs, he was 'to be worshipped through silence alone,' that is, in point of fact, he was not worshipped by the multitude at all...The Babylonians, in their 'popular religion,' supremely worshipped a Goddess Mother and a Son, who was represented in pictures and in images as an infant or child in his mother's arms. From Babylon, the worship of the Mother and the Child spread to the ends of the earth. In Egypt, the Mother and the Child were worshipped under the names of Isis and Osiris. In India, even to this day, as Isi and Iswara; in Asia, as Cybele and Deoius; in Pagan Rome, as Fortuna and Jupiter-puer, or Jupiter, the boy; in Greece, as Ceres, the Great Mother, with the babe at her breast, or as Irene, the goddess of Peace, with the boy Plutus in her arms; and even in Tibet, in China...Shing Moo, the Holy Mother in China, being represented with a child in her arms."* [3]

How is it possible that the teaching that a Son born of a woman is God spread over the whole earth? And how is it possible that the false teaching that the mother is God spread to the whole world?

Colonel J. Garnier wrote, "*There are some modern writers who have represented the various religious superstitions of different nations as being the spontaneous invention of each race, and the natural and uniform outcome of human nature in a state of barbarism. This is not the case ; the theory is wholly opposed to the conclusions of those who have most fully studied the subject. The works of Faber, Sir W. Jones, Pocoke, Hislop, Sir G. Wilkinson, Rawlinson and others have indisputably proved the connection and identity of the religious systems of nations most remote from each other, showing that, not merely Egyptians, Chaldeans, Phoenicians, Greeks and Romans, but also the Hindus, the Buddists of China and Tibet, the Goths, Anglo Saxons,*

Druids, Mexican and Peruvians, the Aborigines of Australia, and even the savages of the South Sea Islands, must have all derived their religious ideas from a common source and centre. Everywhere we see the most startling coincidences in rites, ceremonies, customs, traditions, and in the names and relations of their respective gods and godesses." [4]

The "common source" of the false religion that the mother is God was developed in Babylon after the flood. Then when God confused the languages at Babylon and scattered the people over the face of the earth this false teaching went to the ends of the earth. Only the names were changed due to the fact that new languages were adopted in all the different locations where this false religion was taught.

A more difficult question is what evidence exists that God revealed the truths which lead to the formulating of the false religion concerning a Babylon Madonna and Son? IN other words, is there evidence that those in Babylon received a revelation from God which spoke of the mother and Son since at that time there was no written revelation from God?

End Notes

1. Alexander Hislop, *The Two Babylonians* (Printed in the United States of Anmerica: Chick Publications), 14.

2. *Ibid.*, 16,18.

3. *Ibid.*, 19-20.

4. Colonel J. Garnier, *The Worship of the Dead* (London: Chapman & Hall, Limited, 1904), 3.

Chapter III. The Witness of the Stars

E.W. Bullinger wrote, *"For more that two thousand five hundred years the world was without a written revelation from God. The question is, Did God leave Himself without a witness? The question is answered very positively by the written Word that He did not. In Romans i. 19 it is declared that, 'that which may be known of God is manifest in them ; for God hath shown it to them. For the invisible things of Him from the creation of the world are clearly seen, being understood by the things which were made, even His eternal power and Godhead ; so they are without excuse.' But how was God known? How were His 'invisible things,' i.e., His plans His purposes, and His counsels, known since the creation of the world?...There is only one answer, and that is, THE HEAVENS! This is settled by the fact that the passage is quoted from Ps. xix., the first part of which is occupied with the Revelation of God written in 'the Heavens,' and the latter part of the Revelation of God written in the 'Word.'"* [1]

Here are the verses that Bullinger referenced that are in regard to the revelation of God written in the heavens:

"The heavens declare the glory of God; the skies proclaim the work of his hands. Day after day they pour forth speech; night after night they reveal knowledge. They have no speech, they use no words; no sound is heard from them. Yet their voice goes out into all the earth, their words to the ends of the world" (Ps.19:1-4; NIV).

The Apostle Paul quoted the words *"their voice goes out into all the earth, their words to the ends of the world,"* from Psalm 19:4 when he wrote the following:

"But not all the Israelites accepted the good news. For Isaiah says, 'Lord, who has believed our message?' Consequently, faith comes from hearing the message, and the

message is heard through the word about Christ. But I ask: Did they not hear? Of course they did: 'Their voice has gone out into all the earth, their words to the ends of the world.'" (Ro.10:16-18; NIV).

In his comments on this passage John Nelson Darby wrote the following:

"It is certain that the apostle intends to explain that a proclamation of the truth on God's part had taken place. Israel was without excuse, for the report had even gone out everywhere, the words which announced God unto the ends of the earth. The testimony then was not confined to the Jews. The Gentiles had heard it everywhere." [2]

The word about Christ had gone out into all the earth, and that word is written in the stars. Besides that, the prophets of God have spoken that word "since the world began":

"Blessed be the Lord God of Israel; for he hath visited and redeemed his people, And hath raised up an horn of salvation for us in the house of his servant David; As he spake by the mouth of his holy prophets, which have been since the world began" (Lk.1:68-70).

The prophets of God foretold of a Savior "since the world began." What was the source of this knowledge if it wasn't a revelation from God written in the stars? The following passage also speaks of a Redeemer and Peter said that it was revealed "since the world began":

"Repent ye therefore, and be converted, that your sins may be blotted out, when the times of refreshing shall come from the presence of the Lord; And he shall send Jesus Christ, which before was preached unto you: Whom the heaven must receive until the times of restitution of all things, which God hath spoken by the mouth of all his holy prophets since the world began" (Acts 3:18-21).

In regard to this passage Colonel J. Garnier wrote that "*it is plainly taught, that the prophecy of a redeemer and of the restitution of all things had ever been preached by the signs in the heavens, or by those Stars which God had called by their names, and that their meaning were as plain as if uttered 'in words' or 'by voice,' and being seen all over the world there was no speech nor language where that meaning might not be recognized."* **[3]**

Also, the following passage reveals that even before there was a written revelation from God the prophet Enoch knew about the Lord Jesus' return to the earth spoken of at Acts 3:20:

"Raging waves of the sea, foaming out their own shame; wandering stars, to whom is reserved the blackness of darkness for ever. And Enoch also, the seventh from Adam, prophesied of these, saying, Behold, the Lord cometh with ten thousands of his saints, To execute judgment upon all, and to convince all that are ungodly among them of all their ungodly deeds which they have ungodly committed, and of all their hard speeches which ungodly sinners have spoken against him" (Jude 1:13-15).

God Named the Stars

The Scriptures reveal that God named the stars:

"Lift up your eyes and look to the heavens: Who created all these? He who brings out the starry host one by one and calls forth each of them by name. Because of his great power and mighty strength, not one of them is missing" (Isa.41:26).

God had a purpose in naming the stars and He revealed that name to people to tell a story of things which were coming upon the earth. That is the meaning of the Hebrew word translated "signs" in the following verse:

"And God said, Let there be lights in the firmament of the heaven to divide the day from the night; and let them be for signs, and for seasons, and for days, and years" (Gen.1:14).

One of the meanings of the Hebrew word translated "signs" is "*a sign of something future.*" [4]

The prophecies concerning the coming Redeemer were written in the stars, specifically the "Mazzaroth" found in the following passage where God asked Job if he could do these things:

"*Canst thou bind the sweet influences of Pleiades, or loose the bands of Orion? Canst thou bring forth Mazzaroth in his season? or canst thou guide Arcturus with his sons?*" (Job 38:31-32).

Here the words "Pleiades," "Orion," and "Arcturus" are referring to three different constellations of stars. And the word "Mazzaroth" is referring to "*the signs of the Zodiac.*"[5]

Bullinger says the following about the Twelve Signs of the Zodiac:

"*The Twelve Signs are the same, both as to the meaning of their names and as to their order 'in all the nations of the world.' The Chinese, Chaldean, and Egyptian records go back to more than 2,000 years B.C. Indeed, the Zodiacs in the Temples of Denderah and Esneh, in Egypt, are doubtless copies of Zodiacs still more ancient...Nouet, a french astronomer, infers that the Egyptian Astronomy must have arisen 5,000 B.C...The word 'Zodiac'...denotes a 'way,' or 'step,' and is used of the 'way' or 'path' in which the sun appears to move amongst the stars in the course of the year.*" [6]

"*The figures themselves are perfectly arbitrary,*" says Bullinger, "*There is nothing in the group of stars to even suggest the figures...Take for example the sign of Virgo, and look at the stars. There is nothing whatever to suggest a human form; still less is there anything to show whether that form is a man or woman. And so with all of the others. The 'picture,' therefore, is the original, and must have been drawn around or connected with certain stars, simply in order that it might be identified and associated with them ; and that it might thus be remembered and handed down to posterity...These pictures were designed to preserve, expound, and perpetuate the one first great promise and prophecy of Gen. iii. 15, that all hope for Man, all hope for Creation, was bound up in 'a Coming Redeemer'; One who should be born of a woman ; who would first suffer, and afterwards gloriously triumph ; One who should first be wounded by that great enemy who was the cause of all sin and sorrow and death, but who should finally crush the head of 'that Old Serpent the Devil."* [7]

On the site *Ask the Rabbi* Yirmiyahu Ullman writes that *"the Jewish perspective is that the signs of the zodiac were positioned at the time of Creation, and their influence is intimated in the Torah. Thus our Talmudic Sages describe in great detail the dynamic between the progression of the creation of the zodiac signs and their corresponding influence on Mankind (Pesikta, ch. 4). Furthermore, the entire wisdom of the Torah, including the knowledge of the zodiac, was taught by G-d to Adam and his descendents. Even though it was eventually perverted and incorporated by most of humanity into idol worship, a select few such as Abraham retained its true meaning."* [8]

That explains the existence of representations of the Zodiac in many of the ancient synagogues during the rabbinic period of Jewish history:

"The recurrence of the zodiac in synagogue after synagogue suggests its importance as more than a decorative or ornamental device. Rather, as the talmudic sources make clear and as the continued appearance of the zodiac in later European Jewish art shows, the use of the zodiac in the synagogue of the rabbinic period was consonant with its symbolic importance, an importance that extended from non-Jewish into Jewish metaphysics." [9]

It is also true that the different constellations of the Zodiac represented the twelve tribes of Israel. In the *Jewish Encyclopedia* we read the following:

"*The twelve constellations represent the twelve tribes, while each station of the zodiac has thirty paths, and each path has thirty legions (of stars) (Ber. 32b).*" [10]

Bullinger asks, "*But where are we to 'begin' to read this wondrous Heavenly Scroll? A circle has proverbially neither beginning or end. In what order then are we to consider these signs?...Is not this which is spoken of as the unknown and insoluble mystery--'the riddle of the SPHINX'? The word SPHINX means 'to bind closely together.' It was therefore designed to show where the two ends of the Zodiac were to be joined togeter, and where the great circle of the heavens begins and ends. The SPHINX is a figure with the 'head of a woman' and the 'body of a lion'! What is this but a never-ceasing monitor, telling us to begin with 'Virgo' and to end with 'Leo'! in the Zodiac in the Temple of Esneh, in Egypt, A sphinx is actually placed between the Sign of Virgo and Leo.* [11]

The Mother and Son in the Stars

Joseph A. Seiss wrote that "*these twelve great signs do not stand alone. Each one of them has conjoined with it, either on the north or south side of the Zodiacal belt, three other conspicuous constellations, called Decans, from the Shemitic dek, a 'Part' or 'piece.'*" [12]

Seiss also wrote that one of the decans of the sign of Virgo is "*Coma, the Infant, the Branch, the Desired One.*" [13]

Bullinger wrote that "*The ancient name for this constellation is 'Comah, the desired,' or 'the one longed for.' We have the word used by the Holy Spirit in this very connection, in Hag. ii. 7: 'The DESIRE of all nations shall come'...The ancient Zodiacs pictured this constellation as a woman with a child in her arms. ALBUMAZAR (or ABU MASHER), an Arabian astronomer of the eight century, says, 'There arises in the first Decan, as the Persians, Chaldeans, and Egyptians, and the two HERMES and ASCALIUS teach, 'a young woman,' whose Persian name denotes a pure virgin, sitting on a throne, 'nourishing an infant boy,' (the boy, I say), having a Hebrew name, by some nations called IHESU, with the signification IEZA, which in Greek is called CHRISTOS.'"* [14]

That is the evidence that proves that those in Babylon received a revelation from God which spoke of the mother and Son even before there was a written revelation from God. Next, it will be shown that the truths revealed in the Zodiac by God were perverted.

End Notes

1. E. W. Bullinger, *The Witness of the Stars* (Grand Rapids, MI: Kregel Classics, Reprint of the 1893 ed.), 2-3).

2. John Nelson Darby, *Darby's Bible Synopsis*; Accessed July 8, 2020, https://biblehub.com/commentaries/darby/romans/10.htm

3. Colonel J. Garnier, *The Worship of the Dead* (London: Chapman & Hall, Limited, 1904), 251.

4. *Gesenius' Hebrew-Chaldee Lexicon*, Accessed July 8, 2020, https://www.blueletterbible.org/lang/lexicon/lexicon.cfm?Strongs=H226&t=KJV.

5. *Ibid.*, Accessed July 8, 2020, https://www.blueletterbible.org/lang/lexicon/lexicon.cfm?Strongs=H4216&t=KJV.

6. E. W. Bullinger, *The Witness of the Stars*, 9,15.

7. *Ibid.*, 17,19.

8. *Ask the Rabbi*,"The Zodiac"; Accessed September 15,2010, https://ohr.edu/explore_judaism/ask_the_rabbi/ask_the_rabbi/2394.

9. "Astrology in the Ancient Synagogue," *My Jewish Learning*; Accessed September 15, 2020, https://www.myjewishlearning.com/article/astrology-in-the-ancient-synagogue/

10. "ZODIAC," *Jewish Encyclopedia,*: Accessed September 15, 2020, http://www.jewishencyclopedia.com/articles/15277-zodiac

11. E. W. Bullinger, *The Witness of the Stars* 21-22.

12. Joseph A. Seiss, *The Gospel in the Stars: or, Primeval Astronomy* (Philadelphia, PA: E. Claxton & Company, 1882), 11.

13. *Ibid.*, 12.

14. E. W. Bullinger, *The Witness of the Stars*, 34-35.

Chapter IV. The Perversion of the Zodiac

Nimrod

The following verse speaks of the facts concerning Nimrod and Babylon:

"*Cush became the father of Nimrod; he was the first on earth to be a mighty man. He was a mighty hunter before the Lord; therefore it is said, 'Like Nimrod a mighty hunter before the Lord.' The beginning of his kingdom was Babel, Erech, and Accad, all of them in the land of Shinar*" (Gen.10:8-10; RSVCE).

In *The Companion Bible* we read the following:

"*Josephus (Ant. Jud. i. c. 4. 2) says: 'Nimrod persauded mankind not to ascribe their happiness to God, but to think that his own excellency was the source of it. And he soon changed things into a tyranny, thinking there was no other way to wean men from the fear of God, than by making them rely upon his own power.'*

"*The Targum of Jonathan says: 'From the foundation of the world none was ever found like Nimrod, powerful in hunting, and in rebellions against the Lord.'*

"*The Jerusalem Targum says: 'He was powerful in hunting and in wickedness before the Lord, for he was a hunter of the sons of men, and he said to them, 'Depart from the judgment of the Lord, and adhere to the judgment of Nimrod!' ...The Chaldee paraphrase of 1 Chronicles 1:10 says: 'Cush begat Nimrod, who began to prevail in wickedness, for he shed innocent blood, and rebelled against Jehovah'...We cannot fail to see, in Nimrod, Satan's first attempt to raise up a human universal ruler of men.*" [1]

John Walvoord wrote, "*Nimrod, who founded Babylon,*

(Genesis 10:8-12), had a wife known as Semiramis, who founded the secret religious rites of the Babylonian mysteries, according to accounts outside the Bible. Semiramis had a son with an alledged miraculous conception who was given the name Tammuz and in effect was a false fulfillment of the promise of the seed of the woman given to Eve (Gen. 3:15)." [2]

Semiramis as Virgin

The following is in regard to the myths surrounding Nimrod and Semiramis:

I. A. Sadler wrote, "*The violent death of Nimrod led to a suppression of the false religion. However, it was revived in secret by his wife Semiramis. She claimed that Nimrod was now a god in the form of the sun, of which his earthly representation was fire. She later gave birth to a child, who was supposedly the reincarnation of the hero Nimrod, now the sun god. The child is known under various names, of which one of the most important names is 'Tammuz.' The false claim was made that this was the promised seed of the woman. However, in reality it was an imposture of the Devil, as Semiramis was effectively an harlot and a most evil woman.*" [3]

Legend has it that Nimrod was worshipped as the Sun God. Steven Merrill wrote, "*Myths from civilizations of antiquity describe the sun god (deified Nimrod) fathered Tammuz using a sunbeam to impregnate the maiden Semiramis. The result was a re-incarnated Nimrod. Mythology portrays Semiramis as married to god and mother of that same god*" [4]

Merrill wrote that "Mythology portrays Semiramis as married to god and mother of that same god." Hislop sheds more light on this subject, writing the following: "*This also accounts for the origin of the very same confusion of relationship between Isis and Osiris, the mother and child of the Egyptians; for as Bunsen shows, Osiris was represented in Egypt as at once the son and husband of his mother; and actually bore, as one of his titles of dignity and honor, the name 'Husband of the Mother.' This still further casts light on the fact already noticed, that the Indian God Iswara is represented as a babe at the breast of his own wife Isi, or Parvati."* [5]

Merrill wrote that the sun god, Nimrod, "fathered Tammuz using a sunbeam to impregnate the maiden Semiramis" and Hislop wrote, *"Almost all the Tartar princes trace their genealogy to a celestial virgin, impregnated by a sun-beam, or some equally miraculous means."* [6]

Semiramis was known as the embodiment of lust and licentiousness and Hislop said the following about her:

"The Chaldean Mysteries can be traced up to the days of Semiramis, who lived only a few centuries after the flood, and who is known to have impressed upon them the image of her own depraved and polluted mind. That beautiful but abandoned queen of Babylon was not only herself a paragon of unbridled lust and licentiousness, but in the Mysteries which she had a chief hand in forming, she was worshipped as Rhea, the great 'MOTHER' of the gods." [7]

Therefore, Satan had to wait until her true nature had faded from people's memories before he could portray Semiramis as a virgin. *"As time wore away,"* according to Hislop, *"and the facts of Semiramis's history became obscured, her son's birth was boldly declared to be miraculous : and therefore, she was called 'Alma Mater,' 'the Virgin Mother.' That the birth of the Great Deliverer was to be miraculous, was widely known before the Christian era. For centuries, some say for thousands of years before that event, the Buddist priests had a tradition that a 'Virgin' was to bring forth a child to bless the world."* [8]

The truth that the Deliverer was to be born of a Virgin

was revealed in the stars since almost from the beginning of people's existence on the earth. Bullinger wrote the following about the "sign Virgo, the Promised Seed of the woman:

"Here is the commencement of all prophecy in Gen. iii. 15, spoken to the serpent: 'I will put enmity between thee and the woman, and between thy seed and her seed : it shall bruise thy head, and thou shall bruise His heel.' This is the prophetic announcement which the Revelation in the heavens...is designed to unfold and devolope. It lies at the root of all the ancient traditions and mythologies, which are simply the perversions and corruption of primitive truths.

"VIRGO is represented as a woman with a ' branch' in her right hand, and some ears of corn in her left hand. Thus giving a two-fold testimony of the Coming One. The name of this sign in the Hebrew is 'Bethulah,' which means a 'virgin'; and 'virga', which means 'a branch' (Vulg. Isa. xi.i)." [9]

It is difficult to understand how people could actually believe these myths but Sir Robert Anderson offers the following to explain this phenomenon:

"In no other sphere save that of religion do men of intelligence and culture willingly subject their minds to delusions. The 'historic Church' once tried to compel belief that this planet was the fixed centre of the solar system; but who believes it now? Men cannot be made to believe that water runs uphill, or that five and five make anything but ten. In no other sphere can they be induced to stultify reason and common sense. But in religion there seems to be no limit to their credulity. And in every age, and in all kinds of different environments, credulity fastens, and feeds itself, upon errors and superstitions of a kindred type." [10]

Semiramis as the Third Person of the Assyrian Trinity

Hislop wrote that *"in the Babylonian system...Bacchus went down to hell, rescued his mother from the infernal powers, and carried her with him in triumph to heaven...Now, when the mother of the Pagan Messiah came to be celebrated as having been thus 'Assumed,' then it was that, under the name of the 'Dove,' she was worshipped as the Incarnation of the Spirit of God, with whom she was identified."* 11

In regard to Semiramis, Hislop says that *"Every quality of gentleness and mercy was regarded as centered in her ; and when death had closed her career, while she was fabled to have been deified and changed into a pigeon, to express the celestial benignity of her nature, she was called by the name of 'D'Iune,' or 'The Dove,' or without the article, 'Juno'--the name of the Roman 'queen of heaven,' which has the very same meaning; and under the form of a dove as well as her own, she was worshipped by the Babylonians."* 12

Hislop continues, writing that *"when the deified mother was represented as a Dove, what could the meaning of this representation be but just to identify her with the Spirit of all grace, that brooded, dove-like, over the deep at the creation; for in the sculptures at Nineveh, as we have seen, the wings and tail of the dove represented the third member of the idolatrous Assyrian trinity. In confirmation of this view, it must be stated that the Assyrian 'Juno,' or 'The Virgin Venus,' as she was called, was identified with the 'air.' Thus Julius Firmicus says: 'The Assyrians and part of the Africans wish the air to have the supremacy of the elements, for they have consecrated this same [element] under the name of Juno, or the Virgin Venus.' Why was 'air' thus identified with Juno, whose symbol was that of the third person of the Assyrian trinity? Why, but because in Chaldee the same word which signifies the air signifies also the 'Holy Ghost.'"* 13

"The dove, the chosen symbol of this deified queen," says Hislop, *"is commonly represented with an olive branch in her mouth, as she herself in her human form also is seen bearing the olive branch in her hand; and from this form of*

representing her, it is highly probable that she has derived the name by which she is commonly known, for 'Z'emir-amit' means 'The branch-bearer.'" [14]

Again, Bullinger wrote that the sign of "*VIRGO is represented as a woman with a 'branch' in her right hand.*"

It is not difficult to understand what the "branch" signifies with the following verse in view:

"*Behold, the days come, saith the LORD, that I will raise unto David a righteous branch, and a King shall reign and prosper, and shall execute judgment and justice in the earth*" (Jer.23:5).

Nimrod as the Centaur

Hislop writes, "*The Centaur is found on coins struck in Babylonia...the Centaur is found in the Zodiac, the antiquity of which goes up to a high period, and which had its origin in Babylon. The Centaur was represented, as we are expressly assured by Berosus, the Babylonian historian, in the temple of Babylon, and his language would seem to show that so also it had been in primeval times...But we have seen that Kronos was the first King of Babylon, or Nimrod; consequently, the first Centaur was the same. Now, the way in which the Centaur was represented on the Babylonian coins, and in the Zodiac, viewed in this light, is very striking. The Centaur was the same as the sign Sagittarius, or 'The Archer.'*" [15]

Barry Setterfield wrote, "*Sagittarius is depicted as a Centaur with a bow and arrow pointed towards Antares, the heart of the Scorpion. A Centaur, envisaged as half man half horse, represents a two-natured person. There was only one Person in existence who genuinely had two natures, both God and Man - Jesus Christ.*" [16]

Nimrod as the Slayer of the Serpent

According to Hislop, "*The Greeks represented their great god Apollo as slaying the serpent Pytho, and Hercules as strangling serpents while yet in his cradle. In Egypt, in India, in Scandinavia, in Mexico, we find clear allusions to the same great truth. 'The evil genius,' says Wilkinson, 'of the adversaries of the Egyptian god Horus is frequently figured under the form of a snake, whose head he is seen piercing with a spear. The same fable occurs in the religion of India, where the malignant serpent Calyia is slain by Vishnu, in his avatar of Crishna ; and the Scandinavian deity Thor was said to have bruised the head of the great serpent with his mace.*" [17]

This is a perversion of the meaning of the "Sign Leo (The Lion)."

As noted earlier, the Riddle of the Sphinx it that its Head is Virgo and its Body is Leo. So the last sign represents the Lord's triumph over Satan. "*There is no confusion about 'this' sign,*" according to Bullinger, "*In the ancient Zodiacs of Egypt (Denderah, Esneh) and India we find the Lion....The Hebrew name of the sign is "Arieh,' which means 'the Lion.' There are six Hebrew words for Lion, and this one is used of the Lion 'hunting down his prey.' The Syriac name is 'Aryo, the rending Lion,' and the Arabic is 'Al Asad' ; both mean a 'lion coming vehemently, leaping forth as a flame'...his feet are over the head of 'Hydra,' the great Serpent, and just about to descend upon it and crush it.*" [18]

The Lord Jesus is called the Lion of the tribe of Judah:

"*And one of the elders saith unto me, Weep not: behold, the Lion of the tribe of Judah, the Root of David, hath prevailed to open the book, and to loose the seven seals thereof*" (Rev.5:5).

The following prophecy foretells of the coming of the Lion of the tribe of Judah:

"*he shall eat up the nations his enemies, and shall break their bones, and pierce them through with his arrows. He couched, he lay down as a lion, and as a great lion: who shall stir him up?*" (Num.24:8-9).

As Bullinger says, The Lion's "*feet are over the head of the great Serpent, and just about to descend upon it and crush it.*"

The following verse refers to great Serpent trying to flee from being crushed:

"*By his Spirit the heavens are adorned; his hand hath formed the fleeing serpent*" (Job 26:13).

In his commentary on this verse Albert Barnes wrote, "*His hand hath formed the crooked serpent - Or, rather, the fleeing serpent. There can be no doubt that Job refers here to one of the constellations, which it seems was then known as the serpent or dragon.*" [19]

In regard to the perversion of the teaching found in the Zodiac Colonel J. Garnier wrote that the pagan religion was "*founded on perversion of the truth, its founders would be certain, when perverting and incorporating that truth into their system, to make use of those recognised prophetic signs in the heavens to obtain fictitious credit for their religion. Hence, instead of regarding them as signs by which God had revealed to man the future redemption, they associated them with their false gods, and thus hid from mankind their spiritual meaning.*" [20]

Next, it will be shown that the successor to the Babylonian Mysteries is the church at Rome. Sadler wrote:

"*Despite the fearful flood and destruction of the world, which showed the judgements of God, man soon fell away from the truth. Noah was a preacher of righteousness, but his son Ham was profane. The gracious promise of a saviour, the Messiah, was perverted. Men soon claimed that the promised*

Seed had come, but they claimed that he was Nimrod the founder of Babylon. From the death and supposed reincarnation of Nimrod as the sun god were born the Babylonian Mysteries...the true successor to the Mysteries is the Church of Rome." [21]

Alexander Hislop said, "*It can be proved that the idolatry of the whole earth is one, that the sacred language of all nations is radically Chaldean--that the GREAT GODS of every country and clime are called by Babylonian names-- and that all the Paganisms of the human race are only a wicked and deliberate, but yet most instructive corruption of the primeval gospel first preached in Eden, and through Noah, afterwards conveyed to all mankind. The system, first concocted in Babylon, and thence conveyed to the ends of the earth, has been modified and diluted in different ages and countries. 'In Papal Rome only is it now found nearly pure and entire.'*" [22]

End Notes

1. *The Companion Bible, King James Version* (Grand Rapids, MI: Kregel Publications, 1990), Appendix # 28, 29.

2. John F. Walvoord, "Revelation," in *The Bible Knowledge Commentary; New Testament* ed, by John F. Walvoord & Roy B. Zuck (Colorado Springs, CO: ChariotVictor Publishing, 1983), 970.

3. I. A. Sadler, *Mystery, Babylon the Great; Volume 1* (Chippenham, England, Published by the Author, 2014), 10.

4. Steven Merrill MD, *Nimrod: Darkness in the Cradle of Civilization* (Xulon Press, 2004), 336.

5. Alexander Hislop, *The Two Babylons*, 22-23.

6. *Ibid.*, 305.

7. *Ibid.*, 5.

8. *Ibid.*, 76-77.

9. E. W. Bullinger, *The Witness of the Stars*, 29-30.

10. Sir Robert Anderson, *The Bible or the Church?* Second Edition, (London: Pickering & Inglis), 61.

11. Alexander Hislop, *The Two Babylons*, 125-126.

12. *Ibid.*, 78-79.

13. *Ibid.*, 79.

14. *Ibid.*

15. *Ibid.*, 42.

16. Barry Setterfield, *Is There a Gospel in the Stars?* Accessed July 8, 2020, http://www.setterfield.org/stargospel.html#sagittarius)

17. Alexander Hislop, *The Two Babylons*, 60.

18. E. W. Bullinger, *The Witness of the Stars*, 162,164.

19. Albert Barnes, *Notes, Critical, Illustrative, and Pratical, on the BOOK OF JOB*; Vol.ii. (London: George Routledge, 1847). 51.

20. Colonel J. Garnier, *The Worship of the Dead*, 252.

21. I. A. Sadler, *Mystery, Babylon the Great; Volume 1* , 7.

22. Alexander Hislop, *The Two Babylons*, 224.

Chapter V. Mystery, Babylon the Great

The Mother of Harlots

"And upon her forehead was a name written, MYSTERY, BABYLON THE GREAT, THE MOTHER OF HARLOTS AND ABOMINATIONS OF THE EARTH" (Rev.17:5).

This speaks of the mystery religion which originated in Babylon. In the following verse which speaks of the same mother of harlots we can know that in the future this false religion will prevail over the whole earth:

"And there came one of the seven angels which had the seven vials, and talked with me, saying unto me, Come hither; I will shew unto thee the judgment of the great whore that sitteth upon many waters" (Rev.17:1).

The whore will sit upon "many waters" and that is referring to the whole earth:

"And he saith unto me, The waters which thou sawest, where the whore sitteth, are peoples, and multitudes, and nations, and tongues" (Rev.17:15).

The whore will have her headquarters in the city of seven mountains or seven hills:

Seven Hills

"And the angel said unto me, Wherefore didst thou marvel? I will tell thee the mystery of the woman, and of the beast that carrieth her, which hath the seven heads and ten horns....And here is the mind which hath wisdom. The seven heads are seven mountains, on which the woman sitteth" (Rev.17:7,9).

Dave Hunt wrote the following: *"Here is no mythical or allegorical language but an unambiguous statement in plain* words: 'The woman...is that great city.' There is no justification for seeking some other hidden meaning... Furthermore, she is a city built on 'seven hills.' That specification eliminates ancient Babylon. Only one city has for more than 2000 years been known as the city of seven hills. That city is Rome. The 'Catholic Encyclopedia' states: 'It is within the city of Rome, called the city of seven hills, that the entire area of the Vatican State proper is now confined.'" [1]

Alexander Hislop concurs, writing the following:

"There never has been any difficulty in the mind of any enlightened Protestant in identifying the woman 'sitting on seven mountains,' and having on her forehead the name written, 'Mystery, Babylon the Great,' with the Roman apostacy. No other city in the world has ever been celebrated, as the city of Rome has, for its situation on seven hills. Pagan poets and orators, who had not thought of elucidating prophecy, have alike characterised it as 'the seven hilled city.' Thus Virgil refers to it: 'Rome has both become the most beautiful (city) in the world, and alone has surrounded for herself seven heights with a wall.' Propertius, in the same strain, speaks of it (only adding another trait, which completes the Apocalyptic picture) as 'The lofty city on seven hills, which governs the whole world.' Its 'governing the whole world' is just the counterpart of the Divine statement--'which reigneth over the kings of the earth' (Rev 17:18). To call Rome the city 'of the seven hills' was by its citizens held to be as descriptive as to call it by its own proper name. Hence Horace speaks of it by reference to its seven hills alone, when he addresses, 'The gods who have set their affections on the seven hills.' Martial, in like manner, speaks of 'The seven dominating mountains.' In times long subsequent, the same kind of language was in current use; for when Symmachus, the prefect of the city, and the last acting Pagan Pontifex Maximus, as the Imperial substitute, introduces by letter one friend of his to another, he calls him

'De septem montibus virum'--'a man from the seven mountains,' meaning thereby, as the commentators interpret it, *'Civem Romanum, A Roman Citizen.'* Now, while this characteristic of Rome has ever been well marked and defined, it has always been easy to show, that the Church which has its seat and headquarters on the seven hills of Rome might most appropriately be called 'Babylon,' inasmuch as it is the chief seat of idolatry under the New Testament, as the ancient Babylon was the chief seat of idolatry under the Old." [2]

The Liturgy as Mystery

We read the following in the *Catechism of the Catholic Church*:

"*Liturgical catechesis aims to initiate people into the mystery of Christ (It is 'mystagogy.') by proceeding from the visible to the invisible, from the sign to the thing signified, from the 'sacraments' to the 'mysteries.' Such catechesis is to be presented by local and regional catechisms. This Catechism, which aims to serve the whole Church in all the diversity of her rites and cultures, will present what is fundamental and common to the whole Church in the liturgy as mystery and as celebration (Section One), and then the seven sacraments and the sacramentals (Section Two).*" [3]

Dave Hunt says, "*As for 'Mystery,' that name imprinted on the woman's forehead is the perfect designation for Vatican City. Mystery is the very heart of Roman Catholicism, from the words 'Mysterium fide' pronounced at the alledged transformation of the bread and wine into the literal body and blood of Christ to the enigmatic apparitions of Mary around the world. Every sacrament, from baptism to extreme unction, manifests the mysterious power which the faithful must believe the priests yield, but for which there is no visible evidence.*" [4]

Golden Cup in Her Hand

"And there came one of the seven angels which had the seven vials, and talked with me, saying unto me, Come hither; I will shew unto thee the judgment of the great whore that sitteth upon many waters. With whom the kings of the earth have committed fornication, and the inhabitants of the earth have been made drunk with the wine of her fornication...And the woman was arrayed in purple and scarlet colour, and decked with gold and precious stones and pearls, having a golden cup in her hand full of abominations and filthiness of her fornication" (Rev.17:1-2,4).

This is referring to Babylon:

"Babylon hath been a golden cup in the LORD'S hand, that made all the earth drunken: the nations have drunken of her wine; therefore the nations are mad" (Jer. 51:7).

Pope Leo XII identified the woman with a golden cup in her hand with the church at Rome:

"In 1825, on occasion of the jubilee, Pope Leo XII struck a medal, bearing on the one side his own image, and on the other, that of the Church of Rome symbolized as a 'Woman,' holding in her left hand a cross, and in her right a CUP, with the legend around her, 'Sedet super universum,' 'The whole world is her seat.'" [5]

Drunken With the Blood of the Saints

"And I saw the woman drunken with the blood of the saints, and with the blood of the martyrs of Jesus: and when I saw her, I wondered with great admiration" (Rev.17:6).

Dave Hunt wrote, *"Nineteenth-century Roman Catholic author du Pin writes: 'The pope [Innocent III] and the prelates were of opinion that it was lawful to make use of force, to see whether those who were not reclaimed out of a sense of their salvation might be so by the fear of punishments, and even of temporal death.' Almost everyone knows that crusades were organized of tens of thousands of knights and foot soldiers to retake Jerusalem from the Muslims. Very few have ever heard that similar crusades involving huge armies were fought against Christians who could not in good conscience submit to Rome. Yet such was the case, beginning with Pope Innocent III. A major crime of these Christians was believing in freedom of conscience and worship-biblical concepts which the popes hated, for such beliefs would put Rome out of business. Though no exact figures are available, the slaughter of these Christians by the popes probably ran into the millions during the thousand years before the Reformation. In the city of Beziers alone about 60,000 men, women, and children were wiped out in one crusade. Innocent III considered the annihilation of these particular heretics the 'crowning achievement of his papacy'!"* [6]

Of Pagan Origin

"*T.W. Rhys Davids wrote that the earliest missionaries to Tibet observed that similarities have been seen since the first known contact: 'Lamaism with its shaven priests, its bells and rosaries, its images and holy water, its popes and bishops, its abbots and monks of many grades, its processions and feast days, its confessional and purgatory, and its worship of the double Virgin, so strongly resembles Romanism that the first Catholic missionaries thought it must be an imitation by the devil of the religion of Christ.*" [7]

John Henry Cardinal Newman wrote, "*We are told in various ways by Eusebius, that Constantine, in order to recommend the new religion to the heathen, transferred into it the outward ornaments to which they had been accustomed in their own. It is not necessary to go into a subject which the diligence of Protestant writers has made familiar to most of us. The use of temples, and these dedicated to particular saints, and ornamented on occasions with branches of trees; incense, lamps, and candles; votive offerings on recovery from illness; holy water; asylums; holydays and seasons, use of calendars, processions, blessings on the fields; sacerdotal vestments, the tonsure, the ring in marriage, turning to the East, images at a later date, perhaps the ecclesiastical chant, and the Kyrie Eleison, are all of pagan origin, and sanctified by their adoption into the Church"* [8]

Cardinal Newman also said, "*Confiding then in the power of Christianity to resist the infection of evil, and to transmute the very instruments and appendages of demon-worship to an evangelical use, and feeling also that these usages had originally come from primitive revelations and from the instinct of nature, though they had been corrupted; and that they must invent what they needed, if they did not use what they found; and that they were moreover possessed of the very archetypes, of which paganism attempted the shadows; the rulers of the Church from early times were prepared, should the occasion arise, to adopt, or imitate, or sanction the existing rites and customs of the populace, as well as the philosophy of the educated class.*" [9]

Cardinal Newman said that the early church adopted the rites or customs of the populace and one of those rites was Lent.

Lent

In the *Catechism of the Catholic Church* we read that "by the solemn forty days of Lent the Church unites herself each year to the mystery of Jesus in the desert":

"*Jesus' temptation reveals the way in which the Son of God is Messiah, contrary to the way Satan proposes to him and the way men wish to attribute to him. This is why Christ vanquished the Tempter for us: 'For we have not a high priest who is unable to sympathize with our weaknesses, but one who in every respect has been tested as we are, yet without sinning.' By the solemn forty days of Lent the Church unites herself each year to the mystery of Jesus in the desert.*" (CCC # 540). [10]

Alexander Hislop writes, *"The forty days' abstinence of Lent was directly borrowed from the worshippers of the Babylonian goddess. Such a Lent of forty days, 'in the spring of the year,' is still observed by the Yezidis or Pagan Devil-worshippers of Koordistan, who have inherited it from their early masters, the Babylonians. Such a Lent of forty days was held in spring by the Pagan Mexicans, for thus we read in Humboldt, where he gives account of Mexican observances: 'Three days after the vernal equinox...began a solemn fast of forty days in honour of the sun.' Such a Lent of forty days was observed in Egypt, as may be seen on consulting Wilkinson's Egyptians. This Egyptian Lent of forty days, we are informed by Landseer, in his Sabean Researches, was held expressly in commemoration of Adonis or Osiris, the great mediatorial god."* [11]

"Among the Pagans", says Hislop, *"this Lent seems to have been an indispensable preliminary to the great annual festival in commemoration of the death and resurrection of Tammuz, which was celebrated by alternate weeping and rejoicing, and which, in many countries, was considerably later than the Christian festival, being observed in Palestine and Assyria in June, therefore called the 'month of Tammuz'; in Egypt, about the middle of May, and in Britain, some time in April. To conciliate the Pagans to nominal Christianity, Rome, pursuing its usual policy, took measures to get the Christian and Pagan festivals amalgamated, and, by a complicated but skilful adjustment of the calendar, it was found no difficult matter, in general, to get Paganism and Christianity--now far sunk in idolatry--in this as in so many other things, to shake hands."* [12]

Easter

In the *Catechism of the Catholic Church* we read the following:

"For this reason the Church, especially during Advent and Lent and above all at the Easter Vigil, re-reads and re-

lives the great events of salvation history in the "today" of her liturgy. But this also demands that catechesis help the faithful to open themselves to this spiritual understanding of the economy of salvation as the Church's liturgy reveals it and enables us to live it" (CCC # 1095). [13]

Alexander Hislop says, "*Then look at Easter. What means the term Easter itself? It is not a Christian name. It bears its Chaldean origin on its very forehead. Easter is nothing else than Astarte, one of the titles of Beltis, the queen of heaven, whose name, as pronounced by the people Nineveh, was evidently identical with that now in common use in this country. That name, as found by Layard on the Assyrian monuments, is Ishtar.*" [14]

The Rite of Water Baptism

Sir Robert Anderson notes the changes which took place in regard to the rite of water baptism in the church at Rome when compared to the way that it was practiced in the Scriptures--- "*See, here is water; what doth hinder me to be baptized?*":

"*The first point is the change of name.*

"*(a) So early as the time of Justin Martyr we find a name given to baptism which comes straight from the Greek mysteries - the name 'enlightenment.' It came to be the constant technical term.*

"*(b) The name 'seal,' which also came from the mysteries and from some forms of foreign cult, was used partly of those who had passed the test and who were 'consignati,' as Tertullian calls them, partly of those who were actually sealed upon the forehead in sign of a new ownership.*

"*(c) The term musterion is applied to baptism, and with it comes a whole series of technical terms unknown to the Apostolic Church, but well known to the mysteries, and explicable only through ideas and usages peculiar to them.*"

"The second point is the change of 'time,' which involves a change of conception," says Anderson, *"Instead of baptism being given immediately upon conversion, it came to be in all cases postponed by a long period of preparation."* [15]

Anderson says that those changes were copied from the Eleusinian Mysteries, whose chief shrine was at Eleusis, a city some fourteen miles from Athens.

The following describes the process of water baptism in the church at Rome:

"The period of the catechumenate varies depending on how much the catechumen has learned and how ready he feels to take the step of becoming a Christian. However, the catechumenate typically lasts less than a year...The initiation itself usually occurs on the Easter Vigil, the evening before Easter Day. That evening a special Mass is celebrated at which the catechumens are baptized, then given confirmation, and finally receive the Holy Eucharist. At this point the catechumens become Catholics and are received into full communion with the Church." [16]

Infant Baptism

Rome teaches that because children are tainted by original sin then it is necessary for them to be baptized with water:

"Born with a fallen human nature and tainted by original sin, children also have need of the new birth in Baptism to be freed from the power of darkness and brought into the realm of the freedom of the children of God, to which all men are called" (CCC # 1250).[17]

Anderson wrote, *"The early corrupters of Christianity transferred to their new religion a rite with which their old religion had made them familiar, and this they described by the term which Holy Scripture provided...In Prescott's 'Conquest of Mexico' a description is given of the rite in use* in that country when the Spaniards landed on its shores. The priestess midwife sprinkled water on the head of the infant, and then, after exorcising the unclean spirit (as does the Roman priest), she used these words: 'He now liveth anew and is born anew; now he is purified and cleansed.'

"And in his work on Buddhism Sir Monier Williams describes a similar rite practised in Tibet and Mongolia. The child is baptized on the third or tenth day after birth. 'The priest consecrates the water, while candles and incense are burning. He then dips the child three times, blesses it, and gives it a name.' It was not from Greece that these superstitious rites were derived. All had a common origin, and that origin is to be sought in the mysteries of ancient Babylon." [18]

Pontifex Maximus

Dave Hunt writes, " *When Emperor Constantine supposedly became a Christian in A.D. 313 (really a clever political maneuver), he gave freedom to Christians as well as official status alongside paganism to the Christian church. Since the church was now a recognized religious body in the empire, Constantine, as emperor, had to be acknowledged as its de facto head. As such, he convened the first ecumenical council, the Council of Nicea, in A.D. 325, set its agenda, gave the opening speech, and presided over it as Charlemagne would over the Council of Chalon 500 years later, Interested not in the truth of the gospel but in unifying the empire, Constantine was the first ecumenist and introduced that error into the persecution-wearied church. While heading the Christian church, Constantine continued to head the pagan priesthood, to officiate at pagan celebrations, and to endow pagan temples even after he began to build Christian churches. As head of the pagan priesthood he was the Pontifex Maximus and needed a similar title as head of the Christian church. The Christians honored him as 'Bishop of Bishops,' while Constantine called himself Vicarius Christi, Vicar of Christ. He meant that he was 'another Christ' acting in the place of Christ... In the Middle Ages, the bishops of Rome began to claim that they were the sole representatives of Christ upon earth. Demanding that the entire church worldwide must be subject to their rule, they forbade any other bishops to be called 'papa' or pope and took to themselves the three titles of Constantine-Pontifex Maximus, Vicar of Christ, and Bishop of Bishops-which they retain to this day."* [19]

John Walvoord wrote, "*After the Persians took over Babylon in 539 B.C., they discouraged the continuation of the mystery religions of Babylon. Subsequently the Babylonian cultists moved to Pergamum (or Pergamos) where one of the seven churches of Asia Minor was located (cf. Rev. 2:12-17). Crowns in the shape of a fish head were worn by the chief priests of the Babylonian cult to honor the fish god. The crowns bore the words 'Keeper of the Bridge,' symbolic of the 'bridge' between man and Satan. The handle was adopted by the Roman emperors, who used the Latin title 'Pontifex Maximus,' which means 'Major Keeper of the Bridge.' And the same title was later used by the bishops of Rome. The pope today is often called the 'pontiff,' which comes from 'pontifex.' When the teachers of the Babylon mystery religions later moved from Pergamun to Rome, they were influential in paganizing Christianity...Babylon then is the symbol of apostasy and blasphemous substitution of idol-worship for the worship of God in Christ.*" [20]

Purgatory

Hislop writes, "*In every system, therefore, except that of the Bible, the doctrine of a purgatory after death, and prayers for the dead, has always been found to occupy a place. Go wherever we may, in ancient/or modern times, we shall find that Paganism leaves hope after death for sinners, who, at the time of their departure, were consciously unfit for the abodes of the blest. For this purpose a middle state has* been feigned, in which, by means of purgatorial pains, guilt unremoved in time may in a future world be purged away, and the soul be made meet for final beatitude." [21]

Rome teaches that those who die in God's grace must undergo purification:

"*All who die in God's grace and friendship, but still imperfectly purified, are indeed assured of their eternal salvation; but after death they undergo purification, so as to achieve the holiness necessary to enter the joy of heaven*" (CCC # 1030).[22]

"*The Church gives the name Purgatory to this final purification of the elect, which is entirely different from the punishment of the damned. The Church formulated her doctrine of faith on Purgatory especially at the Councils of Florence and Trent. The tradition of the Church, by reference to certain texts of Scripture, speaks of a cleansing fire: As for certain lesser faults, we must believe that, before the Final Judgment, there is a purifying fire. He who is truth says that whoever utters blasphemy against the Holy Spirit will be pardoned neither in this age nor in the age to come. From this sentence we understand that certain offenses can be forgiven in this age, but certain others in the age to come*" (CCC "# 1031).[23]

According to Paul "to die is gain":

"*For to me to live is Christ, and to die is gain*" (Phil. 1:21; RSV Catholic Edition).

If Rome is right and when a saved person dies he is subjected to a purifying fire then it would make no sense for Paul to say that "to die is gain."

In the following verse Paul makes it plain that being "away from the body" is to be "at home with the Lord":

"*We are of good courage, and we would rather be away

from the body and at home with the Lord" (2 Cor. 5:8; RSVCE).

Paul says practically the same thing in the following passage:

"*If it is to be life in the flesh, that means fruitful labor for me. Yet which I shall choose I cannot tell. I am hard pressed between the two. My desire is to depart and be with Christ, for that is far better*" (Phil. 1:22-23; RSVCE).

Here Paul is speaking of two different things, one being to remain on the earth and continue his service (fruitful labor) for the Lord and the other is to depart (die), which will result in being with Christ.

Paul makes it abundantly clear that when a saved person dies he goes immediately to be with the Lord Jesus in heaven then it is impossible that when a saved person dies he goes to a so-called place called purgatory.

Besides that, the author of the book of Hebrews wrote that Christians have been sanctified through the offering of the body of Jesus Christ and that those who have been sanctified in that way are "perfected for all time":

"*And by that will we have been sanctified through the offering of the body of Jesus Christ once for all...For by a single offering he has perfected for all time those who are sanctified*" (Heb.10:10,14; RSVCE).

When a person is saved he is "made us alive together with Christ":

"*But God, who is rich in mercy, out of the great love with which he loved us, even when we were dead through our trespasses, made us alive together with Christ*" (Eph.2:4-5; RSVCE).

When the elect is made allive "together" with Christ his life is "in the Son":

"And this is the testimony, that God gave us eternal life, and this life is in his Son" (1 Jn.5:11; RSVCE).

That is why Paul says that the Christian's life is hid with Christ:

"For you have died, and your life is hid with Christ in God" (Col. 3:3; RSVCE).

Since Christians are "perfected for all time" it is obvious that they are are not just "imperfectly purified," as Rome teaches, and do not need the purifying fires of a so-called place called "purgatory."

The Worship pf Moloch

Alexander Hislop wrote, *"As the Father of the gods, he was, as we have seen, called Kronos; and every one knows that the classical story of Kronos was just this, that, 'he devoured his sons as soon as they were born.' Such is the analogy between type and antitype. This legend has a further and deeper meaning; but, as applied to Nimrod, or 'The Horned One,' it just refers to the fact, that, as the representative of Moloch or Baal, infants were the most acceptable offerings at his altar...Diodorus Siculus states that the Carthaginians, on one occasion, when besieged by the Sicilians, and sore pressed, in order to rectify, as they supposed, their error in having somewhat departed from the ancient custom of Carthage, in this respect, hastily 'chose out two hundred of the noblest of their children, and publicly sacrificed them' to this god. There is reason to believe that the same practice obtained in our own land in the times of the Druids. We know that they offered human sacrifices to their bloody gods. We have evidence that they made 'their children pass through the fire to Moloch,' and that makes it highly probable that they also offered them in sacrifice; for, from Jeremiah 32:35, compared with Jeremiah 19:5, we find that these two things were parts of one and the same system. The god whom the Druids worshipped was Baal, as the blazing Baal-fires show, and the last-cited passage proves that children were offered in sacrifice to Baal. When 'the fruit of the body' was thus offered, it was 'for the sin of the soul.' And it was a principle of the Mosaic law, a principle no doubt derived from the patriarchal faith, that the priest must partake of whatever was offered as a sin-offering (Num 18:9,10). Hence, the priests of Nimrod or Baal were necessarily required to eat of the human sacrifices; and thus it has come to pass that 'Cahna-Bal,' the 'Priest of Baal,' is the established word in our own tongue for a devourer of human flesh."* [24]

Hislop compares the flagellations practiced in the church at Rome as being "fit for the worship of Moloch":

"Everyone has heard of the Flagellants, who publicly scourge themselves on the festivals of the Roman Church, and who are regarded as saints of the first water. In the early ages of Christianity such flagellations were regarded as purely and entirely Pagan...On Good Friday, at Rome and Madrid, and other chief seats of Roman idolatry, multitudes flock together to witness the performances of the saintly whippers, who lash themselves till the blood gushes in streams from every part of their body. They pretend to do this in honour of Christ, on the festival set apart professedly to commemorate His death, just as the worshippers of Osiris did the same on the festival when they lamented for his loss. The priests of Cybele at Rome observed the same practice. But can any man of the least Christian enlightenment believe that the exalted Saviour can look on such rites as doing honour to Him, which pour contempt on His all-perfect atonement, and represent His most 'precious blood' as needing to have its virtue supplemented by that of blood drawn from the backs of wretched and misguided sinners? Such offerings were altogether fit for the worship of Moloch; but they are the very opposite of being fit for the service of Christ." [25]

The Sign of the Cross

According to Hislop "*There is yet one more symbol of the Romish worship to be noticed, and that is the sign of the cross. In the Papal system as is well known, the sign of the cross and the image of the cross are all in all. No prayer can be said, no worship engaged in, no step almost can be taken, without the frequent use of the sign of the cross...The same sign of the cross that Rome now worships was used in the Babylonian Mysteries, was applied by Paganism to the same magic purposes, was honored with the same honors. That which is now called the Christian cross was originally no Christian emblem at all, but was the mystic Tau of the Chaldeans and Egyptians--the true original form of the letter T--the initial of the name of Tammuz.*"

Hislop continues, writing that "*this Pagan symbol seems first to have crept into the Christian Church in Egypt, and generally into Africa. A statement of Tertullian, about the middle of the third century, shows how much, by that time, the Church of Carthage was infected with the old leaven. Egypt especially, which was never thoroughly evangelised, appears to have taken the lead in bringing in this Pagan symbol. The first form of that which is called the Christian Cross, found on Christian monuments there, is the unequivocal Pagan Tau, or Egyptian 'Sign of life.'*"[26]

Queen of Heaven

In another vein, Hislop writes that "*The primeval promise that the 'seed of the woman should bruise the serpent's head,' naturally suggested the idea of a miraculous birth. Priestcraft and human presumption set themselves wickedly to anticipate the fulfillment of that promise; and the Babylonian queen seems to have been the first to whom that honor was given. The highest titles were accordingly bestowed upon her. She was called the 'queen of heaven.'*" [27]

The following verse is describing Israelites who had

reverted to paganism during the time of the prophet Jeremiah:

"The children gather wood, and the fathers kindle the fire, and the women knead their dough, to make cakes to the queen of heaven, and to pour out drink offerings unto other gods, that they may provoke me to anger." (Jer.7:18).

The following demonstrates that Rome recognizes Mary as "The Queen of Heaven":

Pope Pius XII declared that *"From the earliest ages of the catholic church a Christian people, whether in time of triumph or more especially in time of crisis, has addressed prayers of petition and hymns of praise and veneration to the Queen of Heaven."* [28]

Hislop adds the following: *"The Madonna of Rome, then, is just the Madonna of Babylon. The 'Queen of Heaven' in the one system is the same as the 'Queen of Heaven' in the other. The goddess worshipped in Babylon and Egypt as the Tabernacle or Habitation of God, is identical with her who, under the name of Mary, is called by Rome 'The HOUSE consecrated to God,' 'the awful Dwelling-place,' 'the Mansion of God,' the 'Tabernacle of the Holy Ghost,' the 'Temple of the Trinity.'"* [29]

End Notes

1. Dave Hunt, *A Woman Rides the Beast*, 67.

2. Alexander Hislop, *The Two Babylons*, 1-2.

3. *Catechism of the Catholic Church*, PART TWO, THE CELEBRATION OF THE CHRISTIAN MYSTERY, # 1075.

4. Dave Hunt, *A Woman Rides the Beast*, 68.

5. Alexander Hislop, *The Two Babylons*, 6.

6. Dave Hunt, *A Woman Rides the Beast*, 256.

7. *Encyclopedia Britannica*, 1878 edition, article "Buddhism" by T.W. Rhys Davids.

8. John Henry Cardinal Newman, *An Essay on the Development of Christian Doctrine*; Chapter 8, Section 6.

9. John Henry Cardinal Newman, *An Essay on the Development of Christian Doctrine*; Chapter 8, Section 5.

10. *Catechism of the Catholic Church*, PART ONE, SECTION TWO, CHAPTER TWO, ARTICLE 3, Paragraph 3, # 540.

11. Alexander Hislop, *The Two Babylons*, 104-105.

12. *Ibid.*, 105.

13. *Catechism of the Catholic Church*, PART TWO, SECTION ONE, CHAPTER ONE, ARTICLE 1, # 1095.

14. Alexander Hislop, *The Two Babylons*, 103.

15. Sir Robert Anderson, *The Bible or the Church*, 122.

16. *Catholic Answers*, "How to Become a Catholic"; Accessed July 9, 2020, https://www.catholic.com/tract/how-to-become-a-catholic

17. *Catechism of the Catholic Church*, PART TWO,

SECTION TWO, CHAPTER ONE, ARTICLE 1, # 1250.

18. Sir Robert Anderson, *The Bible or the Church*, 125-126.

19. Dave Hunt, *A Woman Rides the Beast*, 46.

20. John F. Walvrood, "Revelation," in *The Bible Knowledge Commentary; New Testament*, 970-971.

21. Alexander Hislop, *The Two Babylons*, 167.

22. *Catechism of the Catholic Church*, PART ONE, SECTION TWO, CHAPTER THREE, ARTICLE 12, # 1030.

23. *Ibid.*, # 1031.

24. Alexander Hislop, *The Two Babylons*, 155-156.

25. *Ibid.*, 154.

26. *Ibid.*, 201.

27. *Ibid.*, 77.

28. AD CAELI REGINAM, ENCYCLICAL OF POPE PIUS XII, October 11, 1954.

29. Alexander Hislop, *The Two Babylons*, 83.

Chapter VI. Satan Blinds the Minds of Unbelievers

Beginning in this chapter and continuing for the next five chapters the false teaching of the church at Rome will be answered by the Scriptures. When the Lord Jesus was tempted by Satan He always quoted the Scriptures in order to answer Satan's taunts:

"Being forty days tempted of the devil. And in those days he did eat nothing: and when they were ended, he afterward hungered. And the devil said unto him, If thou be the Son of God, command this stone that it be made bread. And Jesus answered him, saying, It is written, That man shall not live by bread alone, but by every word of God. And the devil, taking him up into an high mountain, shewed unto him all the kingdoms of the world in a moment of time. And the devil said unto him, All this power will I give thee, and the glory of them: for that is delivered unto me; and to whomsoever I will I give it. If thou therefore wilt worship me, all shall be thine. And Jesus answered and said unto him, Get thee behind me, Satan: for it is written, Thou shalt worship the Lord thy God, and him only shalt thou serve. And he brought him to Jerusalem, and set him on a pinnacle of the temple, and said unto him, If thou be the Son of God, cast thyself down from hence: For it is written, He shall give his angels charge over thee, to keep thee: And in their hands they shall bear thee up, lest at any time thou dash thy foot against a stone. And Jesus answering said unto him, It is said, Thou shalt not tempt the Lord thy God. And when the devil had ended all the temptation, he departed from him for a season" (LK.4:2-13).

Now let us look at the following passage:

"But if our gospel be hid, it is hid to them that are lost: In whom the god of this world hath blinded the minds of them

which believe not, lest the light of the glorious gospel of Christ, who is the image of God, should shine unto them" (2 Cor.4:3-4).

The "glorious gospel of Christ" spoken of here is the "gospel of the grace of God":

"*But none of these things move me, neither count I my life dear unto myself, so that I might finish my course with joy, and the ministry, which I have received of the Lord Jesus, to testify the gospel of the grace of God*" (Acts 20:24).

Here is what Rome teaches in regard to how people are saved:

"*The Council of Trent teaches that the Ten Commandments are obligatory for Christians and that the justified man is still bound to keep them; the Second Vatican Council confirms: 'The bishops, successors of the apostles, receive from the Lord . . . the mission of teaching all peoples, and of preaching the Gospel to every creature, so that all men may attain salvation through faith, Baptism and the observance of the Commandments.'*" (CCC # 2068). [1]

According to Rome no one can be saved unless they observe the Ten Commandments. On the other hand, the gospel of grace teaches that salvation is secured by faith alone apart from observing the commandmants. Rome puts a wrong meaning on the word "law" in the following passage:

"*For no human being will be justified in his sight by works of the law, since through the law comes knowledge of sin*" (Ro.3:20; RSV Catholic Edition).

Here the words "no human being" must include both Gentiles and Jews. So the words "the law," which refer to the Law of Moses, cannot be a correct translation since the Gentiles were never given the Law of Moses:

"*When Gentiles who have not the law do by nature what*

the law requires, they are a law to themselves, even though they do not have the law. They show that what the law requires is written on their hearts, while their conscience also bears witness and their conflicting thoughts accuse or perhaps excuse them" (Ro.2:14-15; RSV Catholic Edition).

Since the Gentiles do not have the Law of Moses then the following is the correct translation of Romans 3:20:

"*wherefore by works of law shall no flesh be declared righteous before Him, for through law is a knowledge of sin*" (Ro.3:20; Young's Literal Translation).

We read, "*through law is a knowledge of sin.*" In regard to the Gentiles the law which is a knowledge of sin is the moral law. That is the only law to which the conscience bears witness.

In regard to the Jews it is the Ten Commandments which is a knowledge of sin, as witnessed by the following words of Paul found later in the same epistle:

"*What then shall we say? That the law is sin? By no means! Yet, if it had not been for the law, I should not have known sin. I should not have known what it is to covet if the law had not said, 'You shall not covet.'*" (Ro.7:7; RSV Catholic Edition).

The law which says, "You shall not covet," is one of the Ten Commandments (Ex.20:17).

So at Romans 3:20 Paul is saying that by the moral law shall no flesh be declared righteous in the sight of God, and that moral law must include the Ten Commandments. Despite this Rome teaches that "*all men may attain salvation through faith, Baptism and the observance of the Commandments.*" Next, let us look at the following passage which is also speaking of both the Gentiles and the Jews:

"*therefore do we reckon a man to be declared righteous*

by faith, apart from works of law. The God of Jews only is He, and not also of nations? yes, also of nations; since one is God who shall declare righteous the circumcision by faith, and the uncircumcision through the faith" (Ro.3:28-30; YLT).

Here Paul is saying a person is declared righteous by faith, apart from the moral law. Again, Rome declares that no one can be saved apart from the moral law, the Ten Commandments:

"*The Council of Trent teaches that the Ten Commandments are obligatory for Christians and that the justified man is still bound to keep them; the Second Vatican Council confirms: 'The bishops, successors of the apostles, receive from the Lord . . . the mission of teaching all peoples, and of preaching the Gospel to every creature, so that all men may attain salvation through faith, Baptism and the observance of the Commandments.'*" (CCC 2068).

How does Rome defend this teaching in view of what Paul wrote at Romans 3:28-30?

Jimmy Akin is the Senior Apologist at "Catholic Answers," a contributing editor to "Catholic Answers Magazine," and a weekly guest on "Catholic Answers Live." He wrote the following about the Romans 3:28-30:

"*A passage of crucial importance is Romans 3:28-30, where we read: 'For we hold that a man is justified by faith apart from works of the Law. Or is God the God of Jews only? Is he not the God of Gentiles also? Yes, of Gentiles also, since God is one; and he will justify the circumcised on the ground of their faith and the uncircumcised through their faith.' It is of decisive importance to recognize what Law Paul is talking about here. Unfortunately, most Protestants never ask that question but simply assume one way or another without looking at any evidence beyond the preaching they have heard. Fortunately, Paul answers the question for us immediately after stating that we are justified by faith (in Christ) and not by works of the Law he immediately asks, 'Or is God the God of the Jews only?' Well, what Law do Jews have that Gentiles don't? The Mosaic Law. He then makes the same point in the next statement, saying that God will justify the circumcised and the uncircumcised by faith. Okay, what Law commands circumcision? Again, the Mosaic Law."* **2**

Akin says that "the works of the law" are referring to circumcision and he also says that these "works" also refer to the ceremonial laws of the Mosaic Covenant, writing that "*Paul clearly has the ceremonial works in mind but he does not clearly have the moral work in mind.*" **3**

Despite the fact that the "works of law" are referring to the moral law Akin teaches that the law in question is circumcision and the ceremonial law.

Paul also wrote the following:

"*For Christ is an end of law for righteousness to every one who is believing*" (Ro.10:4; YLT)

Despite the fact that Paul says that "*Christ is an end of law for righteousness to every one who is believing*" the followers of the church at Rome are taught that they must establish their own righteousness. Paul makes it plain that is a serious error:

"*I bear them witness that they have a zeal for God, but it is not enlightened. For, being ignorant of the righteousness that comes from God, and seeking to establish their own, they did not submit to God's righteousness*" (Ro.10:2; RSV Catholic Edition).

The Apostle Paul makes it plain that a believer is justified "freely" by God's grace:

"*Being justified freely by his grace through the*

redemption that is in Christ Jesus" (Ro.3:24).

Paul also made it plain that eternal life is a gift of God, writing that "*the gift of God is eternal life through Jesus Christ our Lord*" (Ro.6:23).

Those who have the spirit which is of God know the things which are "freely" given to them:

"*Now we have received, not the spirit of the world, but the spirit which is of God; that we might know the things that are freely given to us of God*" (1 Cor.2:12).

It is obvious that the church at Rome and her followers do not have the spirit which is of God because they believe that one cannot be saved apart from doing the works of the law and there is nothing free when it comes to salvation.

Faith Alone

According to the Lord Jesus the only thing which is necessary to receive eternal life is "believing":

"*Very truly I tell you, the one who believes has eternal life*" (Jn.6:47).

The Lord Jesus said that those who believe have eternal life. And the following words of Peter confirm that believers already possess eternal life:

"*And this is the record, that God hath given to us eternal life, and this life is in his Son*" (1 Jn.5:11).

Here is what the Lord Jesus said about those to whom He gives eternal life:

"*And I give unto them eternal life; and they shall never perish, neither shall any man pluck them out of my hand*" (Jn.10:28).

These facts are confirmed here:

"*For God so loved the world that he gave his one and only Son, that whoever believes in him shall not perish but have eternal life*" (Jn.3:16; NIV).

At Romans 6:23 we read that "*the gift of God is eternal life*" and Paul says that *"the gifts and calling of God are without repentance"* (Ro.11:29), meaning that once He bestows the gift of eternal life He will not take back that gift. The Christian is saved and will remain saved because he believed the gospel of the grace of God.

Also, the Lord Jesus said the following to the woman who annointed His feet with oil:

"*And he said unto her, Thy sins are forgiven. And they that sat at meat with him began to say within themselves, Who is this that forgiveth sins also? And he said to the woman, Thy faith hath saved thee; go in peace*" (Lk.7:48-50).

The Lord did not tell the woman that her faith and her works had saved her but instead He told her that "Thy faith hath saved thee." Paul and other believers who were with him answered the question as to how a person can be saved in the following way:

"*And brought them out, and said, Sirs, what must I do to be saved? And they said, Believe on the Lord Jesus Christ, and thou shalt be saved, and thy house*" (Acts 16:30-31).

Did Paul and all of those believers just forget to add other things which are necessary for salvation? Of course not! They all knew that the gospel is the power of salvation to all who believe:

"*For I am not ashamed of the gospel of Christ: for it is the power of God unto salvation to every one that believeth*" (Ro.1:16).

Faith

What do the Scriptures say about the word "faith" as used in the following verse?:

"*Therefore we conclude that a man is justified by faith without the deeds of the law*" (Ro.3:28).

Here is what the author of the book of Hebrews says about the word faith:

"*Now faith is the substance of things hoped for, the evidence of things not seen*" (Heb.11:1).

Those with saving faith have the "evidence" of things not seen. As Paul said, "*And my speech and my preaching was not with enticing words of man's wisdom, but in demonstration of the Spirit and of power: That your faith should not stand in the wisdom of men, but in the power of God*" (1 Cor.2:4-5).

Saving faith stands in the power of God and those with true faith have the evidence that the revelation from God is true. So when Paul says that we conclude that a man is justified by faith without the deeds of the law then those with true faith know that it is true. So when the Lord Jesus said the following He was saying that those who "believe" have a faith that stands in the power of God:

"*Very truly I tell you, the one who believes has eternal life*" (Jn.6:47).

How is it possible for anyone to think that it takes more than believing to be saved since the Lord Jesus only mentioned one thing? Would anyone dare assert that He just forgot to mention something else that is needed to obtain eternal life? How could anyone deny that the Lord Jesus was saying that eternal life in the Son comes by "faith alone"?

Jommy Akin does deny it, writing that "*if we are to conform our language to the language of the Bible, we need to reject usage of the formula 'faith alone' while at the same time preaching that man is justified 'by faith and not by works of the Law' (which Catholics can and should and must and do preach, as Protestants would know if they read Catholic literature). James 2:24 requires rejection of the first formula while Romans 3:28 requires the use of the second.*"[4]

Justification in the Epistle of James

Here is the verse from the epistle of James which Akin cited which he thinks refutes the idea of salvation by faith alone:

"*Ye see then how that by works a man is justified, and not by faith only*" (Jas. 2:24).

Those who follow Rome overlook what James said in the first chapter which tells us exactly how a person is saved:

"*Of his own will begat he us with the word of truth, that we should be a kind of firstfruits of his creatures*" (Jas.1:18).

According to James the new birth comes as a result of believing the word of truth and nothing more. That is the same exact same teaching of Peter here:

"*Being born again, not of corruptible seed, but of incorruptible, by the word of God...And this is the word which by the gospel is preached unto you.*" (1 Pet.1:23,25).

Peter tells these believers that they were born again by the gospel which was preached unto them.

A person is born again by the gospel. So let us look at James 2:24 in its context:

"*Even so faith, if it hath not works, is dead, being alone. Yea, a man may say, Thou hast faith, and I have works: shew me thy faith without thy works, and I will shew thee my faith by my works*" (Jas.2:17-18).

The "dead faith" is not in regard to salvation because it

has already been shown that in the first chapter James said that a person is born again by the gospel which was preached to them. So the dead faith is in regard to something else: *"shew me thy faith without thy works, and I will shew thee my faith by my works"*

If a person says he has faith but has no good works which flow from his faith then in another person's opinion that person's faith is a dead faith. Now let us look at this passage:

"Was not Abraham our father justified by works, when he had offered Isaac his son upon the altar? Seest thou how faith wrought with his works, and by works was faith made perfect?" (Jas.2:21-22).

Here James says that Abraham was justified by works but Paul says that his justification by works was not before God:

"For if Abraham were justified by works, he hath whereof to glory; but not before God" (Ro.4:2).

Since James is speaking what what one person can know about another person's faith then the justification under discussion in the second chapter of James is about a justification before men. And here we read the Lord Jesus speaking about a justification before men:

"And he said unto them, Ye are they which justify yourselves before men; but God knoweth your hearts: for that which is highly esteemed among men is abomination in the sight of God" (Lk.16:15).

John Calvin wrote that the justification in the second chapter in the book of James is "before men": *"That we may not then fall into that false reasoning which has deceived the Sophists, we must take notice of the two fold meaning, of the word justified. Paul means by it the gratuitous imputation of righteousness before the tribunal of God; and James, the manifestationof righteousness by the conduct, and that before men, as we may gather from the preceding words,*

'Shew to me thy faith,' etc." [5]

Sir Robert Anderson wrote, "*The Epistle to the Romans is essentially doctrinal, and the practical is based upon the doctrine. The Epistle to 'the twelve tribes scattered abroad,' is essentially practical, the doctrinal element being purely incidental. Paul's Epistle unfolds the mind and purposes of God, revealing His righteousness and wrath. The Epistle of James addresses men upon their own ground. The one deals with justification as between the sinner and God, the other as between man and man. In the one, therefore, the word is, 'To him that worketh not, but believeth.' In the other it is, 'What is the profit if a man say he hath faith, and have not works?' Not 'If a man have faith,' but 'If a man say he hath faith,' proving that, in the case supposed, the individual is not dealing with God, but arguing the matter with his brethren. God, who searches the heart, does not need to judge by works, which are but the outward manifestation of faith within; but man can judge only by appearances.*" [6]

The Gospel is the Power of God Unto Salvation

The church at Rome denies what Paul wrote here:

"*For I am not ashamed of the gospel of Christ: for it is the power of God unto salvation to every one that believeth*" (Ro.1:16).

Since the gospel is the power of God unto salvation to everyone who believes then it is obvious when a person believes the gospel then he is saved. However, Jimmy Akin writes, "*Paul indicates that eternal life is a reward for "perseverance in good work" (Rom 2:7) and that we "seek . . . immortality by perseverance in good works."* [7]

Here is the verse which Akin cites:

"*For those who aimed for glory and honour and immortality by persevering in doing good, there will be eternal life*" (Ro.2:7; NJB).

If a person "perseveres" in doing good works then he will indeed receive eternal life. The Greek word translated "persevering" means "*a patient enduring, sustaining.*" [8]

That explains the following translation of the same verse:

"*To them who by patient continuance in well doing seek for glory and honour and immortality, eternal life*" (Ro.2:7; KJV).

If a person "continues" in well doing then he will receive eternal life. But if he doesn't continue in well doing and sins then he will not inherit eternal life by his works or deeds.

In summary, Satan blinds the minds of unbelievers to the light of the gospel of grace by giving them a false gospel that says that believers are saved by grace but yet they have to do the work of keeping the commandments. Therefore, those who deceived by this counterfeit gospel never see the light of the true gospel of grace and are never saved:

"*For I am not ashamed of the gospel of Christ: for it is the power of God unto salvation to every one that believeth*" (Ro.1:16).

God wants all men to be saved and come to the knowledge of the truth (1 Tim.2:4) and Satan wants none to be saved and as many as he can deceive he places under a curse:

"*for as many as are of works of law are under a curse, for it hath been written, 'Cursed is every one who is not remaining in all things that have been written in the Book of the Law -- to do them,' and that in law no one is declared righteous with God, is evident*" (Gal.3:10).

Satan places hundreds of millions of people under the curse through the agency of the church at Rome and this will be the fate of those who remain in darkness because of Satan and the church at Rome:

"And to you who are troubled rest with us, when the Lord Jesus shall be revealed from heaven with his mighty angels, In flaming fire taking vengeance on them that know not God, and that obey not the gospel of our Lord Jesus Christ: Who shall be punished with everlasting destruction from the presence of the Lord, and from the glory of his power" (2 Thess.1:7-9).

End Notes

1. *Cathecism of the Catholic Church*, PART THREE, SECTION TWO, # 2068.

2. Jimmy Akin, "Paul and the Law"; Accessed July 9, 2010, https://jimmyakin.com/library/paul-and-the-law

3. Jimmy Akin, "The Works of the Law"; Accessed July 9, 2010, https://www.ewtn.com/catholicism/library/works-of-the-law-1181

4. Jimmy Akin, "Justification by Faith Alone"; Accessed July 9, 2019, https://jimmyakin.com/library/justification-by-faith-alone

5. John Calvin, "Commentary on James"; Accessed July 9, 2020, https://www.ccel.org/ccel/c/calvin/calcom45/cache/calcom45.pdf

6. Sir Robert Anderson, *The Gospel and Its Ministry* (Grand Rapids, MI: Kregel Publications, 1978), 160.

7. Jimmy Akin, "The Works of the Law"; Accessed July 9, 2020, https://www.ewtn.com/catholicism/library/works-of-the-law-1181

8. Joseph Henry Thayer, *A Greek English Lexicon of the New Testament*, 644.

Chapter VII. The Rite of Water Baptism

Romes teaches the following about the rite of water baptism:

"Holy Baptism is the basis of the whole Christian life, the gateway to life in the Spirit ('vitae spiritualis ianua'), and the door which gives access to the other sacraments. Through Baptism we are freed from sin and reborn as sons of God; we become members of Christ, are incorporated into the Church and made sharers in her mission: 'Baptism is the sacrament of regeneration through water in the word.'" (CCC # 1213).[1]

According to Rome a person becomes "reborn as sons of God" when baptized with water. However, The Scriptures reveal that before a person could be water baptized they must first believe, as witnessed by Philip's encounter with the eunuch:

"And as they went on their way, they came unto a certain water: and the eunuch said, See, here is water; what doth hinder me to be baptized? And Philip said, If thou believest with all thine heart, thou mayest. And he answered and said, I believe that Jesus Christ is the Son of God" (Acts 8:36-37).

The eunuch said, *"I believe that Jesus Christ is the Son of God"* so he was born of God and made a son of God before a drop of water touched him:

"Whosoever believeth that Jesus is the Christ is born of God: and every one that loveth him that begat loveth him also that is begotten of him. By this we know that we love the children of God, when we love God, and keep his commandments. For this is the love of God, that we keep his commandments: and his commandments are not grievous. For whatsoever is born of God overcometh the world: and this is the victory that overcometh the world, even our faith. Who is he that overcometh the world, but he that believeth

that Jesus is the Son of God?" (1 Jn.5:1-5).

Acts 2:38

"Then Peter said to them, 'Repent, and let every one of you be baptized in the name of Jesus Christ for the remission of sins; and you shall receive the gift of the Holy Spirit'" (Acts 2:38; NKJV).

Rome uses Acts 2:38 to try to attempt to pervert the purpose of water baptism:

"From the very day of Pentecost the Church has celebrated and administered holy Baptism. Indeed St. Peter declares to the crowd astounded by his preaching: 'Repent, and be baptized every one of you in the name of Jesus Christ for the forgiveness of your sins; and you shall receive the gift of the Holy Spirit.'" (CCC # 1226).[2]

Most people assume that this verse is speaking about salvation because they think that the gift is the Holy Spirit Himself. But it will be shown that the gift is bestowed by the Holy Spirit and that gift is the ability to speak in tongues. On the day of Pentecost believers were in fact given that gift and that gift was given to believers to better "serve" the Lord so Acts 2:38 is not about "salvation" but instead about "service."

The Gift of the Holy Spirit "Poured Out"

The following passage describes the event when Gentiles were first given the gift of the Holy Spirit:

"While Peter was still speaking these words, the Holy Spirit fell upon all those who heard the word. And those of the circumcision who believed were astonished, as many as came with Peter, because the gift of the Holy Spirit had been poured out on the Gentiles also" (Acts 10:44-45; NKJV).

The gift of the Holy Spirit was "poured out" on the Gentiles as it had previously been poured on the Jews and the following verse speaks of that previous "pouring out" of the gift of the Holy Spirit:

"*Therefore being exalted to the right hand of God, and having received from the Father the promise of the Holy Spirit, He poured out this which you now see and hear*" (Acts 2:33; NKJV).

The "gift of the Holy Spirit" was poured out and that same gift was seen and heard on the day of Pentecost. Here is what was seen and heard that day:

"*And there were dwelling at Jerusalem Jews, devout men, out of every nation under heaven. Now when this was noised abroad, the multitude came together, and were confounded, because that every man heard them speak in his own language. And they were all amazed and marvelled, saying one to another, Behold, are not all these which speak Galilaeans? And how hear we every man in our own tongue, wherein we were born?*" (Acts 2:5-8).

Therefore, it is clear that the "gift of the Holy Spirit" of Acts 2:38 was "tongues," which was the ability of believers to speak in languages of which they previously had no knowledge. That is the same gift of the Holy Spirit spoken of here:

"*Now there are diversities of gifts, but the same Spirit. And there are differences of administrations, but the same Lord. And there are diversities of operations, but it is the same God which worketh all in all. But the manifestation of the Spirit is given to every man to profit withal. For to one is given by the Spirit the word of wisdom; to another the word of knowledge by the same Spirit; To another faith by the same Spirit; to another the gifts of healing by the same Spirit; To another the working of miracles; to another prophecy; to another discerning of spirits; to another divers kinds of tongues*" (1 Cor.12:4-10).

One of the "gifts" of the Spirit listed here is the gift of *"diverse kinds of tongues."*

Peter Quotes Joel 2:38

On the day of Pentecost the Apostle Peter said that God's pouring forth of His spirit on that day was a fulfillment of the prophecy of Joel 2:28:

"But this is that which was spoken by the prophet Joel; And it shall come to pass in the last days, saith God, I will pour out of my Spirit upon all flesh: and your sons and your daughters shall prophesy, and your young men shall see visions, and your old men shall dream dreams (Acts 2:16-17).

In his commentary on this passage John Gill wrote: *"By the Spirit is meant the gifts of the Spirit, the spirit of wisdom and knowledge, of understanding the mysteries of the Gospel, of explaining the Scriptures, and of speaking with tongues; and by the pouring of it out, is intended the abundance and great plenty of the gifts and graces of the Spirit bestowed; but yet not all of him, or all his gifts and grace in the large extent of them: therefore it is said, not 'my Spirit.' but 'of my Spirit,' or 'out of it,' as out of an unfathomable, immeasurable, and inexhaustible fountain and fulness."*[3]

What was poured forth and what the Jews saw and heard on the day of Pentecost was believers speaking in tongues. That is what is meant by by the words "And your sons and your daughters shall prophesy" at Acts 2:17. The Greek word translated "prophesy" in some instances is in regard to foretelling the future but the word can also mean *"speak-forth by divine inspirations."*[4]

In his commentary on the Greek word translated "prophesy" at Acts 2:17 Albert Barnes wrote that *"it denotes, then, in general, 'to speak under a divine influence,' whether in foretelling future events, in celebrating the praises of God, in instructing others in the duties of religion, or 'in speaking foreign languages under that influence.' In this last sense the word is used in the New Testament, to denote those who were miraculously endowed with the power of speaking foreign languages."*[5]

Forgiveness of Sins

The Scriptures reveal that there is a forgiveness of sins for those who are already saved. And before anyone could be baptized with water that person must first believe, as witnessed by Philip's encounter with the eunuch:

"And as they went on their way, they came unto a certain water: and the eunuch said, See, here is water; what doth hinder me to be baptized? And Philip said, If thou believest with all thine heart, thou mayest. And he answered and said, I believe that Jesus Christ is the Son of God" (Acts 8:36-37).

Before the eunuch was baptized with water he was already "born of God" because he believed that the Lord Jesus is both the Christ and the Son of God:

"Whosoever believeth that Jesus is the Christ is born of God: and every one that loveth him that begat loveth him also that is begotten of him. By this we know that we love the children of God, when we love God, and keep his commandments. For this is the love of God, that we keep his commandments: and his commandments are not grievous. For whatsoever is born of God overcometh the world: and this is the victory that overcometh the world, even our faith. Who is he that overcometh the world, but he that believeth that Jesus is the Son of God?" (1 Jn.5:1-5).

There can be no doubt that the eunuch was "born again" and saved before he was baptized with water so the rite of water baptism at Acts 2:38 was for those already saved. And the following "forgiveness of sins" is likewise for those who are already saved:

"This then is the message which we have heard of him, and declare unto you, that God is light, and in him is no darkness at all. If we say that we have fellowship with him, and walk in darkness, we lie, and do not the truth..If we confess our sins, he is faithful and just to forgive us our sins, and to cleanse us from all unrighteousness" (1 Jn.1:5-6, 9)

John is saying that if a believer "confesses" his sins then he will be cleansed from the things which interrupt his "fellowship" with the Lord. The baptism of repentance was also in regard to confessing sins:

"In those days came John the Baptist, preaching in the wilderness of Judaea...Then went out to him Jerusalem, and all Judaea, and all the region round about Jordan, And were baptized of him in Jordan, confessing their sins" (Mt.3:1, 5-6).

Repent and Be Baptized

Acts 2:38 was the same "baptism of repentance for the remission of sin" (Mark 1:4) which John the Baptist preached except for the fact that those who submitted to the baptism of Acts 2:38 also received the "gift of the Holy Spirit," the ability to speak in tongues. The purpose of John the Baptist's ministry and the rite of water baptism was "to make ready a people prepared for the Lord":

"And he shall go before him in the spirit and power of Elias, to turn the hearts of the fathers to the children, and the disobedient to the wisdom of the just; to make ready a people prepared for the Lord" (Lk.1:17).

The purpose of John's ministry was to turn the hearts of the Israelites from being disobedient unto having the attitude of righteous people. In order to prepare the children of Israel for the Lord. they were to "repent" (have a change of mind) in regard to the sinful lifestyle they were living.

William Barclay offered the following meaning of the word "repent" as used at Acts 2:38: *"'Repent,' said Peter, 'first and foremost.' What does repentance mean? The word originally meant an 'afterthought.' Often a second thought shows that the first thought was wrong; and so the word came to mean 'a change of mind.' But, if a man is honest, a change of mind demands 'a change of action.' Repentance must involve both change of mind and change of action. A man may change his mind and come to see that his actions were wrong but be so much in love with his old ways that he will not change them."*[6]

When anyone submitted to the rite of water baptism he was pledging to change his way of living for the better. That is why John the Baptist said the following to the Pharisees and Sadducees:

"But when he saw many of the Pharisees and Sadducees come to his baptism, he said unto them, O generation of vipers, who hath warned you to flee from the wrath to come? Bring forth therefore fruits meet for repentance" (Mt.3:7-8).

John the Baptist was telling them that since they were pledging to change their way of living then they should exhibit a real change in their lives.

Conclusion

It has been demonstrated that the "gift of the Holy Spirit" was "poured out" on believers (Acts 10:45) and what was "poured out" was what those on the day of Pentecost saw and heard (Acts 2:33)--believers speaking in tongues. The ability to speak in tongues was given to believers in order that they might be the Lord Jesus' witnesses: *"But ye shall receive power, after that the Holy Ghost is come upon you: and ye shall be witnesses unto me both in Jerusalem, and in all Judaea, and in Samaria, and unto the uttermost part of the earth"* (Acts 1:8)

Therefore, the giving of the gift of the Holy Spirit to believers on the day of Pentecost was for "service" and not for "salvation."

1 Peter 3:20

"Which sometime were disobedient, when once the longsuffering of God waited in the days of Noah, while the ark was a preparing, wherein few, that is, eight souls were saved by water. The like figure whereunto even baptism doth also now save us (not the putting away of the filth of the flesh, but the answer of a good conscience toward God,) by the resurrection of Jesus Christ " (1 Pet.3:20-21).

Not the Putting Away of the Filth of the Flesh

Here Peter speaks of the "baptism" which now saves us, and he says that the baptism that saves us is not "the putting away of the filth of the flesh." The following words of Ananias spoken to Paul are in reference to "putting away the filth of the flesh":

"And now why tarriest thou? arise, and be baptized, and wash away thy sins calling on the name of the Lord" (Acts 22:16).

Sir Robert Anderson writes, *"The Apostle records the words which Ananias addressed to him (Paul) at his conversion: 'Arise and be baptized, and wash away thy sins, calling on the name of the Lord'...His meaning again is clear: 'Arise and be baptized, and turn away from your evil courses, calling on His name.'"*[7]

This is in regard to "putting away the filth of the flesh." It is speaking about practical holiness or "perfecting holiness":

"Having therefore these promises, dearly beloved, let us cleanse ourselves from all filthiness of the flesh and spirit, perfecting holiness in the fear of God" (2 Cor.7:1).

From this we can know that the baptism which saves us is not water baptism.

The Baptism That Saves

The baptism that now saves us is the one baptism into Jesus Christ and into His death:

"Know ye not, that so many of us as were baptized into Jesus Christ were baptized into his death?" (Rom. 6:3).

Being baptized "into Jesus Christ" is the same baptism spoken of here:

"For as many of you as have been baptized into Christ have put on Christ. There is neither Jew nor Greek, there is neither bond nor free, there is neither male nor female: for ye are all one in Christ Jesus" (Gal.3:27-28).

Since there is only one spiritual baptism (Eph.4:5) when a believer is baptized into the Body of Christ (1 Cor.12:13) that same baptism by the Holy Spirit serves to baptize or immerse the believer into the death of the Lord Jesus. His death becomes the death of the believer because the believer takes part in His death.

Lewis Sperry Chafer wrote the following about believers who are "baptized into His death":

"'Know ye not [Or are you ignorant] that so many of us as were baptized into Jesus Christ were baptized into his death?' As certainly we are are 'in Him' we partake of the 'value' of His death. So also the passage states: 'Therefore we are buried with him by baptism into death' (cf. Colossians 2:12). Thus we are actually partakers of His crucifixion (v. 6), death (v. 8), burial (v. 4), and resurrection (vs. 4, 5, 8) and as essentially as we would partake had 'we' been crucified, dead, buried and raised."[8]

Chafer says that the believer partakes in the Lord Jesus' crucifixion. When that happens the Christian is saved because the Lord Jesus paid the penalty for our sins.

The Like Figure

The words "the like figure" are describing a "type". The "water" that bore up the ark and saved Noah is a "type" or "illustration" using things of the physical sphere is teach things in regard to the spiritual sphere.

The Jews would understand that it was the "water" of the flood that bore up the ark and therefore saved Noah and his family. In other words, they were saved by the very thing that brought about death to all the rest of mankind.

So Noah and his family were saved from death by that which brought death. That is also true of the salvation that comes to Christians. For when the believer is baptized into the Body of Christ by the Holy Spirit he becomes one with Christ, even into His death:

"For by one Spirit are we all baptized into one Body...the Body of Christ" (1 Cor.12:13,27).

"Know ye not, that so many of us as were baptized into Jesus Christ were baptized into his death? " (Ro.6:3).

Sir Robert Anderson writes, *"the apostle enforces the symbolism of death by declaring that baptism is the antitype of the Flood. The water which overwhelmed the world bore up the ark. Noah was thus saved from death by death; as is the sinner who on believing in Christ becomes one with Him in death."*[9]

Titus 3:5

"he saved us, not because of righteous things we had done, but because of his mercy. He saved us through the washing (loutron) of rebirth and renewal by the Holy Spirit" (Titus 3:5; NIV).

Rome attempts to use this verse to support their unscriptual teaching that the rite of water baptism is necessary in order to enter the kingdom of God:

"This sacrament is also called 'the washing of regeneration and renewal by the Holy Spirit,' for it signifies and actually brings about the birth of water and the Spirit without which no one 'can enter the kingdom of God.'" (CCC # 1215).[10]

The key to understanding this verse which speaks of the "new birth" is knowing the meaning of the Greek word *loutron,* which is translated as "washing."

Sir Robert Anderson writes, *"The word rendered 'washing' is a noun, not a verb. This loutron is, strictly speaking, not the washing, but the vessel which contains the water. Certain expositors of course wish to read it 'font' or 'laver' ; but this is a false exegesis. The New Testament is written in the language of the Septuagint version of the Old; and we turn to that authority to settle for us the meaning of any doubtful term...And for this purpose the Apocryphal books are sometimes as useful as the sacred Scriptures. Now, loutron is not the rendering for 'laver' in the Greek version. The LXX use it twice; namely in Cant. iv. 2 (where it is the washing place for sheep); and in Ecclesiasticus XXX1. 25, where the Son of Sirach writes: 'He that washeth himself after the touching of a dead body, if he touch it again what avails his loutron?' "*

"This last passage is of the very highest importance here, and gives us the clew we are in search of. The reference is to one of the principal ordinances of the Mosaic ritual - a type, moreover, which fills a large place in New Testament doctrine - especially in Hebrews - namely, the great sin-offering as connected with 'the water of purification' (Numb. xix.)"[11]

The Jew became "unclean" or defiled if he touched a

dead body (Num.19:11). The way to be cleansed was provided under the law, and that way was by the sin-offering of the red heifer (Num.19:2). That sin-offering was killed and then the corpse was burned. Then water that flowed over those ashes was sprinkled upon the defiled person and in that way he became purified (Num.19:17-19).

Here Sir Robert Anderson explains the meaning of the "type" of the "water": "*How could the defiled Israelite gain access to the sacrifice of the great sin-offering for purification? Water which had flowed over the ashes of the sacrifice was sprinkled upon him. We know what the sacrifice typified, what did the water typify? What is the means by which the defiled sinner is brought into contact, as it were, with the great sin-offering of Calvary? By 'the word of the truth of the Gospel.'* "[12]

The following verse demonstrates the validity of Anderson's statement:

"*Husbands, love your wives, even as Christ also loved the church, and gave himself for it; That he might sanctify and cleanse it with the washing (loutron) of water by the word*" (Eph.5:26).

The Greek word *loutron* comes from the word *louo* and the suffix *tron*. The word *louo* means "to bathe, wash." The suffix *tron* is a Greek suffix denoting an "intrument." One of the meanings of the word "instrument" is "utensil, container." Therefore, the Greek word *loutron* can carry with it the meaning of a vessel containing water that has flowed over the sin offering. The following verse speaks of that vessel:

"*Then for the unclean person they shall take some of the ashes of the burnt purification from sin and flowing water shall be added to them in a vessel.*" (Num.19:17).

Therefore, the correct translation of Titus 3:5 is as follows:

"*he saved us, not because of righteous things we had done, but because of his mercy. He saved us through the vessel of rebirth and renewal by the Holy Spirit*" (Titus 3:5; NIV).

Born of Water and the Spirit

In His sermon to Nicodemus the Lord Jesus spoke of regeneration in connection with the "individual" sinner as well as with the "nation" of Israel. He told Nicodemus:

"*I tell you the truth, no one can see the kingdom of God unless he is born again*" (Jn.3:3; NIV).

To this Nicodemus asked how he could be born again when he is old, and the Lord Jesus said: "*I tell you the truth, no one can enter the kingdom of God unless he is born of water and the Spirit. Flesh gives birth to flesh, but the Spirit gives birth to spirit*" (Jn.3:5-6; NIV).

Previously the Lord had been speaking of an individual's regeneration but He now begins to speak of the nation of Israel's regeneration. The Lord shifts from using the second person "singular" pronoun "you" to the second person "plural":

"*You should not be surprised at my saying, 'You must be born again. The wind blows wherever it pleases. You hear its sound, but you cannot tell where it comes from or where it is going. So it is with everyone born of the Spirit*" (Jn.3:7-8; NIV).[A footnote in the NIV at verse seven says, "*The Greek is plural.*"]

From this we can understand that the Lord Jesus was going to use the rebirth of the nation of Israel to illustrate the rebirth of of individuals.

Nicodemus still not understand so he asked, "*How can these things be?*"

By the Lord's reply we can understand that Nicodemus should have been aware of some truth in the OT Scriptures which spoke of a regeneration by the Spirit: "*Art thou a teacher of Israel, and knoweth not these things?*" (v.10).

Nicodemus should have been aware of the prophecies that speak of the blessings of the New Covenant promised to the nation of Israel. In the thirty-sixth chapter of Ezekiel we see "water" being sprinkled on that nation and the Lord putting His Spirit within that nation:

"*For I will take you from among the heathen, and gather you out of all countries, and will bring you into your own land. Then will I sprinkle clean water upon you, and ye shall be clean: from all your filthiness, and from all your idols, will I cleanse you. A new heart also will I give you, and a new spirit will I put within you: and I will take away the stony heart out of your flesh, and I will give you an heart of flesh*" (Ezek. 36:24-26).

In regard to the sprinkling of the water we read the following in the *Jamieson-Fausset-Brown Bible Commentary*: "*sprinkle...water--phraseology taken from the law; namely, the water mixed with the ashes of a heifer sprinkled with a hyssop on the unclean (Nu 19:9-18).*"[13]

Then in the next chapter of Ezekiel, chapter 37, we see the nation of Israel being "born again" or "born of the spirit." Ezekiel was "set down in the midst of the valley which was full of dry bones" (Ezek.37:1) and he was told by God that "*these bones are the whole house of Israel*" (v.11). Then God asked Ezekiel, "*can these bones live?*" Then God told Ezekiel how they will come to life:

"*Then the LORD told me, 'Prophesy to these bones' Tell them: 'You dry bones, listen to the message from the LORD: 'This is what the Lord GOD says to you dry bones!' 'Pay attention! I'm bringing my Spirit into you right now, and you're going to live!*" (Ez.37:5; ISV).

The word "prophesy" in this verse is translated as *propheteuo* in the LXX (the Greek translation of the OT), and that word can refer to foretelling the future but it also means "*to utter forth, declare a thing which can only be known by divine revelation.*" [14]

The following passage speaks of the time when the Lord Jesus will come to Israel and at that time it will be the spirit and the word which will result in the regeneration of the nation of Israel:

"*And the Redeemer shall come to Zion, and unto them that turn from transgression in Jacob, saith the LORD. As for me, this is my covenant with them, saith the LORD; My spirit that is upon thee, and my words which I have put in thy mouth, shall not depart out of thy mouth, nor out of the mouth of thy seed, nor out of the mouth of thy seed's seed, saith the LORD, from henceforth and for ever*" (Isa.59:20-21).

The message of the Lord by which Israel will come to life is the gospel that Jesus is the Christ, the Son of God:

"*And many other signs truly did Jesus in the presence of his disciples, which are not written in this book: But these are written, that ye might believe that Jesus is the Christ, the Son of God; and that believing ye might have life through his name*" (Jn.20:30-31).

Upon believing that message the Jews will be Born of God, which is the same as being born of the Spirit:

"*Whosoever believeth that Jesus is the Christ is born of God: and every one that loveth him that begat loveth him also that is begotten of him. By this we know that we love the children of God, when we love God, and keep his commandments. For this is the love of God, that we keep his commandments: and his commandments are not grievous. For whatsoever is born of God overcometh the world: and this is the victory that overcometh the world, even our faith. Who is he that overcometh the world, but he that believeth that Jesus is the Son of God?"* (1 Jn.5:1-5).

From all of this we can understand that in "type" the nation of Israel will receive her blessings when she experiences her new birth through the "water"--specifically the water of of Numbers 19:9, water which is a purification for sin. On the other hand, in reality all of Israel's blessings will come through the "word."

Here we read that the "water is the word":

"Husbands, love your wives, even as Christ also loved the church, and gave himself for it; That he might sanctify and cleanse it with the washing of water by the word" (Eph.5:26).

In the two following passages we can see that the new birth comes about by believing the gospel:

"He chose to give us birth through the word of truth, that we might be a kind of firstfruits of all he created" (Jas.1:18; NIV).

"Being born again, not of corruptible seed, but of incorruptible, by the word of God...And this is the word which by the gospel is preached unto you" (1 Pet.1:23,25).

Also, the following words of the Lord Jesus demonstrate that the gospel comes in the power of the spirit of God:

"It is the spirit that quickeneth; the flesh profiteth nothing: the words that I speak unto you, they are spirit, and they are life" (Jn.6:63).

Mark 16:16

"He that believeth and is baptized shall be saved; but he that believeth not shall be damned" (Mk.16:16).

Here the Lord is not saying that a requirement for

salvation is baptism with water, but instead He is describing those who will be saved. This is similiar to the following words of the Lord:

"*And every one that hath forsaken houses, or brethren, or sisters, or father, or mother, or wife, or children, or lands, for my name's sake, shall receive an hundredfold, and shall inherit everlasting life*" (Mt.19:29).

Here the Lord says that those who have forsaken their families will receive everlasting life, but surely no one will argue that this is a requirement for salvation. Instead, the Lord is merely describing many who will be saved. Therefore we can understand that at Mark 16:16 the Lord Jesus is merely describing those who will be saved. The words which follow Mark 16:16 demonstrate that the Lord is "describing" those who will be saved:

"*And these signs shall follow them that believe; In my name shall they cast out devils; they shall speak with new tongues; They shall take up serpents; and if they drink any deadly thing, it shall not hurt them; they shall lay hands on the sick, and they shall recover*" (Mk.16:17-18).

Now let us look at the following passage:

"*And all the people that heard him, and the publicans, justified God, being baptized with the baptism of John. But the Pharisees and lawyers rejected the counsel of God against themselves, being not baptized of him*" (Lk.7:29-30).

John D. Grassmick writes, "*Though the New Testament writers generally assume that under normal circumstances each believer will be baptized, 16:16 does not mean that baptism is a necessary requirement for personal salvation. The second half of the verse indicates by contrast that one who does not believe the gospel will be condemned by God (implied) in the day of final judgment (cf. 9:43-48). The basis for condemnation is unbelief, not the lack of any ritual observance...Thus the only requirement for personally appropriating God's salvation is faith in Him."*[15]

The following words of the Lord Jesus demonstrate that Grassmick is correct when he said that "the only requirement for personally appropriating God's salvation is faith in Him":

"Very truly I tell you, the one who believes has eternal life" (Jn.6:47; NIV).

End Notes

1. *Catechism of the Catholic Church*, Part Two, Section Two, Chapter One, Article 1, "The Sacrament of Baptism"; Accessed June 25, 2020, https://www.vatican.va/archive/ccc_css/archive/catechism/p2s2c1a1.htm

2. *Ibid.*

3. John Gill, *Exposition of the Entire Bible*, Commentary at Acts 2:17; Accessed May 7, 2020, https://biblehub.com/commentaries/gill/acts/2.htm.

4. Joseph Henry Thayer, *A Greek-English Lexicon of the New Testament* (Grand Rapids, MI: Baker Book House, 2000), 553.

5. Albert Barnes, *Explanatory and Practical, On The Acts of the Apostles* (New York, NY: Leavitt Lord & Co., 1835), 35.

6. William Barclay, *The Acts of the Apostles*; Revised Edition (Philadelphia, PA: The Westminster Press, 1977), 28-29.

7. Sir Robert Anderson, *The Bible or the Church?*, (London: Pickering and Inglis, Second Edition), 230-231.

8. Lewis Sperry Chafer, *He That Is Spirtual* (Grand Rapids, MI: Zondervan Publishing House, 1967), 122-123.

9. Sir Robert Anderson, *The Bible or the Church?*, 228-229.

10. *Catechism of the Catholic Church*, Part Two, Section Two, Chapter One, Article 1, "The Sacrament of Baptism"; Accessed June 25, 2020, https://www.vatican.va/archive/ccc_css/archive/catechism/p2s2c1a1.htm

11. *Ibid.*, 225.

12. *Ibid.*, 226-27.

13. *Jamieson-Fausset-Brown Bible Commentary,* Accessed June 17, 2020, https://biblehub.com/commentaries/jfb/ezekiel/36.htm

14. Joseph Henry Thayer, *A Greek-English Lexicon of the New Testament*, 553.

15. John D. Grassmick, "Mark," in *The Bible Knowledge Commentary; New Testament*, edited by John Walvoord and Roy Zuck, (Chariot Victor Publishing, 1983), 196.

Chapter VIII. Infant Baptism and Original Sin

Rome teaches that "*Born with a fallen human nature and tainted by original sin, children also have need of the new birth in Baptism to be freed from the power of darkness and brought into the realm of the freedom of the children of God, to which all men are called. The sheer gratuitousness of the grace of salvation is particularly manifest in infant Baptism. The Church and the parents would deny a child the priceless grace of becoming a child of God were they not to confer Baptism shortly after birth*" (CCC # 1250).[1]

The theory of Original Sin, according to the church at Rome, can be summarized by the following statement:

"*Adam and Eve transmitted to their descendants human nature wounded by their own first sin and hence deprived of original holiness and justice; this deprivation is called 'original sin'*" (CCC # 417).[2]

Rome also teaches that the sin of Adam has been transmitted to all people at birth and results in the "death of the soul"

"*Following St. Paul, the Church has always taught that the overwhelming misery which oppresses men and their inclination towards evil and death cannot be understood apart from their connection with Adam's sin and the fact that he has transmitted to us a sin with which we are all born afflicted, a sin which is the 'death of the soul'. Because of this certainty of faith, the Church baptizes for the remission of sins even tiny infants who have not committed personal sin*" (CCC # 403).[3]

Calvinist Thomas R. Schreiner, the James Buchanan Harrison Professor of New Testament Interpretation at the

Southern Baptist Theological Seminary, teaches that the "death of the soul" is referring to "spritual death," writing that "*human beings enter into the world condemned and spiritually dead because of Adam's one sin.*"[4]

Rome says that "*we do know by Revelation that Adam had received original holiness and justice not for himself alone, but for all human nature. By yielding to the tempter, Adam and Eve committed a personal sin, but this sin affected the human nature that they would then transmit in a fallen state. It is a sin which will be transmitted by propagation to all mankind, that is, by the transmission of a human nature deprived of original holiness and justice*" (CCC #404).[5]

It will be shown that all people do not emerge from the womb spiritually dead and in a fallen state and deprived of original holiness and justice.

The Lord Jesus Was Made Like His Brethren in All Things

"*For verily he took not on him the nature of angels; but he took on him the seed of Abraham. Wherefore in all things it behoved him to be made like unto his brethren, that he might be a merciful and faithful high priest in things pertaining to God, to make reconciliation for the sins of the people*" (Heb.2:16-17).

In his commentary on this verse Matthew Poole wrote that "*To be made like unto his brethren; a man having a true body and soul like them in every thing, which was necessary to make him a complete Redeemer; agreeable to them in all things necessary to their nature, qualities, conditions, and affections; like them in sorrows, griefs, pains, death.*"[6]

According to Poole the Lord Jesus' body and soul was just like the body and soul of every person.

Albert Barnes sees the same truth, writing that "*Wherefore in all things - In respect to his body; his soul; his rank and character. There was a propriety that he should be like them, and should partake of their nature."* [7]

It defies reason to argue that all people emerge from the womb with a corrupted nature and spiritually dead despite the fact that the Scriptures reveal that the Lord Jesus was made like His brothers in "all things." However, that is exactly the argument that the advocates of the theory of Original Sin make.

God Created Mankind Upright

"'Look,' says the Teacher, 'this is what I have discovered: Adding one thing to another to discover the scheme of things--while I was still searching but not finding--I found one upright man among a thousand, but not one upright woman among them all. This only have I found: God created mankind upright, but they have gone in search of many schemes'" (Eccl.7:25-29; NIV).

We can understand that here Solomon is speaking of the uprightness of "mankind" and not just the uprightness of only Adam and Eve. Mark Dunagan understands the same truth:

"God made men upright"-i.e. morally good, God created men and women in His own image...God has given to every one the ability to recognize divine law as truth. This explains why Solomon found only one righteous man in a thousand. The failure wasn't due to how God created people, rather, God created mankind upright. Note the verse isn't saying that people are born inherently depraved, rather, after being born, after a period of childhood innocence, most people depart from God and search out excuses for not serving God." [8]

Adam Clarke agrees with Dunagan, writing the following: "*Lo, this only have I found, that God hath made man upright - Whatever evil may be now found among men and women, it is not of God; for God made them all upright. This is a singular verse, and has been most variously translated: "Elohim has made mankind upright, and they have sought many computations."*[9]

Made in the Image of God

The following verse demonstrates that all people are made in the image of God:

"For if the woman be not covered, let her also be shorn: but if it be a shame for a woman to be shorn or shaven, let her be covered. For a man indeed ought not to cover his head, forasmuch as he is the image and glory of God: but the woman is the glory of the man" (1 Cor.11:7).

In this verse the Greek word translated "he is" the image and glory of God is in the "present tense" so the verse is not referring to just Adam being the image and glory of God. Adam Clarke wrote: *"He is the image and glory of God - He is God's vicegerent in this lower world; and, by the authority which he has received from his Master, he is his representative among the creatures, and exhibits, more than any other part of the creation, the glory and perfections of the Creator."*[10]

We can see the same truth here:

"Whoso sheddeth man's blood, by man shall his blood be shed: for in the image of God made he man." (Gen.9:6).

The reason why all murderers are to be put to death is because those murdered are created in the image of God. What is said here would not make any sense if just Adam and Eve were created in the image of God. We also read the following which is in regard to the same truth:

"Therewith bless we God, even the Father; and therewith curse we men, which are made after the similitude of God" (Jas.3:9).

The Greek word translated "curse we" is in the "present" tense so the words about being made after the similitude of God are describing all people and not just Adam and Eve.

Henry Morris wrote that "*This is a reference to Genesis 1:26-27. Even though scarred by thousands of years of sin and the curse, man is still made in the image of God, and should be respected as such.*"[11]

Adam was created in the image of God and according to Him everything He made was "very good" (Gen.1:31). Since all people are created in the image or similitude of God all people emerge from the womb "very good."

That matches perfectly with the way that David said he was made:

"*For you created my inmost being; you knit me together in my mother's womb. I praise you because I am fearfully and wonderfully made; your works are wonderful, I know that full well*" (Ps.139:13-14; NIV).

No one in the history of Christendom has played a larger role in formulating the theory of Original Sin as Augustine of Hippo, and he wrote the following:

"*Our bodies would not have been born with defects, and there would have been no human monsters, if Adam had not corrupted our nature by his sin...The sickly and dying nature of the human body, proceeds from the lapse of the first man.*"[12]

What Augustine said here cannot possibly be correct because David said that he was "wonderfully made."

The Rebirth and Renewing of the Holy Spirit

In the following verse the Apostle Paul describes how he was saved by being made alive by the spirit:

"*He saved us through the washing of rebirth and renewal*

by the Holy Spirit" (Titus 3:5; NIV).

Joseph Henry Thayer says that the Greek word translated 'rebirth' "*denotes the restoration of a thing to its pristine state, its renovation.*"[13]

The word "rebirth" is translated from the Greek word *paliggenesia*, which is the combination of *palin* and *genesis*.

Palin means "*joined to verbs of all sorts, it denotes renewal or repetition of the action.*"[14]

According to BDAG, *palin* refers "*to repetition in the same (or similar) manner, again, once more, anew of something a pers. has already done.*"[15]

Genesis means "*used of birth, nativity.*"[16]

So when we combine the two words the meaning is a repetition of a birth. Therefore, when Paul used the Greek word translated "rebirth" to describe his salvation experience he was speaking of a repetition of a birth.

It is obvious that the reference is not to a "physical" rebirth, or the repetition of one's physical birth. Paul could only be speaking of a repetition of a spiritual birth. And the words that follow make it certain that the "birth" of which Paul is referring to is a "spiritual" birth--"*renewal of the Holy Spirit.*"

Since the renewal of the Holy Spirit is in regard to being made alive spiritually then the previous birth of the Spirit must also be in regard to being made alive spiritually by the Holy Spirit. In other words, since a person is "rebirthed" by the Holy Spirit then that means that one must have previously been born of the Holy Spirit. That happens at conception.

In the following passage Paul speaks of being "alive" before he sinned:

"*For I was alive without the law once: but when the commandment came, sin revived, and I died. And the commandment, which was ordained to life, I found to be unto death. For sin, taking occasion by the commandment, deceived me, and by it slew me*" (Ro.7:9-11).

Paul is not speaking of "physical" death because he was alive physically when he wrote those words. He is speaking about breaking one of the Ten Commandments (v.7) and it was that which resulted in his "spiritual death."

In his commentary on this passage John A. Witmer writes, "*As a result Paul 'died' spiritually (cf. 6:23a) under the sentence of judgment by the Law he had broken...so this sin deceived him...and 'put' him 'to death' (lit., 'killed' him), not physically but spiritually.*"[17]

Since Paul died spiritually when he sinned then he was alive spiritually prior to his sin and therefore he was born of the Spirit when he was conceived in the womb. The Lord Jesus said:

"*That which is born of the flesh is flesh; and that which is born of the Spirit is spirit*" (Jn.3:6).

Besides that, the Scriptures declare that people are created by the LORD when He sends forth His spirit:

"*Thou sendest forth thy spirit, they are created: and thou renewest the face of the earth*" (Ps.104.30).

Elihu told Job the following:

"*The Spirit of God hath made me, and the breath of the Almighty hath given me life*" (Job.33:4).

The fact that all people emerge from the womb spiritually alive completely destroys the theory of Original Sin because according to that theory all people are dead spiritually when they come into the world at birth. Thomas R. Schreiner writes that "*human beings enter the world spiritually dead (and physical death will follow in due course) because of Adam's sin. Human beings do not enter into the world in a neutral state. They are 'dead upon arrival' because of Adam's sin!"*[18]

The Kingdom Belongs to Little Children

The following words of the Lord Jesus about "little children" prove that He did not believe that little children enter the world with a fallen nature:

"Then people brought little children to Jesus for him to place his hands on them and pray for them. But the disciples rebuked them. Jesus said, 'Let the little children come to me, and do not hinder them, for the kingdom of heaven belongs to such as these'" (Mt.19:13-14; NIV).

According to the theory of Original Sin infants and little children emerged from the womb totally depraved and therefore cannot enter the kingdom of God in their fallen state but the Lord says that the kingdom belongs to them. At another place we see the Lord Jesus speaking about children and here the same truth can be seen:

"At the same time came the disciples unto Jesus, saying, Who is the greatest in the kingdom of heaven? And Jesus called a little child unto him, and set him in the midst of them, And said, Verily I say unto you, Except ye be converted, and become as little children, ye shall not enter into the kingdom of heaven. Whosoever therefore shall humble himself as this little child, the same is greatest in the kingdom of heaven" (Mt.18:1-4).

If the idea of Original Sin is correct then we must stand reason on its head and imagine that the Lord Jesus was teaching that unless we become deprived of holiness we cannot enter into the kingdom of heaven! That is patently ridiculous and common sense dictates that the Lord Jesus did not believe that infants come into the world tainted with

Original Sin .

We can also see that children are also described as being "an heritage of the Lord":

"*Lo, children are an heritage of the LORD: and the fruit of the womb is his reward*" (Ps.127:3).

Despite these facts Rome teaches that an infant must be baptized with water to be freed from the power of darkness:

"*Born with a fallen human nature and tainted by original sin, children also have need of the new birth in Baptism to be freed from the power of darkness and brought into the realm of the freedom of the children of God, to which all men are called*" (CCC # 220).[19]

All People Are Born Spiritually Alive

In order to understand that all people are born spiritually alive let us look first at the following verse :

"*And you did he make alive, when ye were dead through your trespasses and sins*" (Eph.2:1; ASV).

A note at Ephesians 2:5 in *The Scofield Study Bible* states that "*Spiritual death is the state of the natural or unregenerate person still in his sins (2:1), alienated from the life of God (4:18-19), and destitute of the Spirit...*" [20]

In *The Pulpit Commentary* we read that "*the death ascribed to the Ephesians in their natural state is evidently spiritual death, and 'trespasses and sins,' being in the dative seems to indicate the cause of death - 'dead through your trespasses and your sins' (R.V.)*" [21]

From this we can understand that a person dies spiritually as a result or because of his own sin, and not as a result of Adam's sin. Therefore, before a person sins and dies spiritually he was alive spiritually.

In his commentary of the passage at Ephesians 2:1 R.C. Sproul writes that "*in this passage Paul speaks of the Spirit's work in 'quickening' us or regenerating us from our fallen condition. He uses the image of being 'made alive.' This is set in stark contrast to our former condition of being 'dead' in tresspasses and sins. The sinner is not biologically dead. Indeed the natural man is very much alive. Corpses do not sin. The death in view here is clearly spiritual death.*" [22]

Sproul recognizes the fact that when a person sins then he dies spiritually, which can only mean that before a person sins he is alive spiritually. We also read the following commentary on Ephesians 2:1 in *The Expositor's Greek Testament*:

"*Here sin is that which makes dead--the cause of the death-state. In the kindred passage in Col. ii. 13 we have the same idea expressed.*" [23]

With this in mind we will look at Colossians 2:13:

"*And you, being dead through your trespasses and the uncircumcision of your flesh, you, I say, did he make alive together with him, having forgiven us all our trespasses*" (Col.2:13; ASV).

In *Vincent's Word Studies* we read the following: "*In your sins...the dative is instrumental, through or by.*" [24]

At Colossians 2:13 Paul is telling these people that they are dead on account of or as a result of their own sins. And the "death" spoken of in the following passage must be in regard to a person's own sins resulting in spiritual death:

"*When tempted, no one should say, 'God is tempting me.' For God cannot be tempted by evil, nor does he tempt anyone; but each person is tempted when they are dragged away by their own evil desire and enticed. Then, after desire has conceived, it gives birth to sin; and sin, when it is full-grown, gives birth to death*" (Jas.1:13-15).

It is a fact that in order for a person to die spiritually when he sins then that person must first be alive spiritually. And the following words of the Lord Jesus make it plain that once a person believes and is made alive spiritually he will never die spiritually:

"*I am the resurrection, and the life: he that believeth in me, though he were dead, yet shall he live: And whosoever liveth and believeth in me shall never die*" (Jn.11:25-26).

Joseph Benson wrote the following commentary on John 11:26:

"*To the soul: he who, being united to Christ by faith, lives a spiritual life by virtue of that union, shall never die; his spiritual life shall never be extinguished, but perfected in eternal life.*" [25]

The life which the Lord Jesus bestows on believers is spiritual life (Jn.3:6, Jn.6:63) and the believer will never die spiritually so the words of James at 1:13-15 cannot be in regard to believers dying spiritually. The only alternative is that all people die spiritually when they sin because all people emerge from the womb spiritually alive and not spiritually dead.

Despite the clear facts that a person dies spiritually as a result of his personal sins Rome asserts that the "death of the soul" is a result of Adam's sin:

"*Following St. Paul, the Church has always taught that the overwhelming misery which oppresses men and their inclination towards evil and death cannot be understood apart from their connection with Adam's sin and the fact that he has transmitted to us a sin with which we are all born afflicted, a sin which is the 'death of the soul'.*" (CCC # 403) [26]

The Riddle of Romans 5:12-19

Thomas Schreiner says Romans 5:12-19 serves as the basis for denying or affirming original sin:

"Whether Scripture teaches what is traditionally called 'original sin' depends significantly on the exegesis of Romans 5:12-19. Since the days of Augustine, the interpretation of this text functions as the basis for denying or affirming original sin. I will argue in this chapter that the most plausible reading of Romans 5:12-19, both exegetically and theologically, supports the doctrine of original sin and original death." [27]

Rome also quotes these verses in an attempt to affirm the theory of Original Sin:

"All men are implicated in Adam's sin, as St. Paul affirms: 'By one man's disobedience many (that is, all men) were made sinners': 'sin came into the world through one man and death through sin, and so death spread to all men because all men sinned.' The Apostle contrasts the universality of sin and death with the universality of salvation in Christ. 'Then as one man's trespass led to condemnation for all men, so one man's act of righteousness leads to acquittal and life for all men.'" (CCC # 402).[28]

Rome speaks of "the universality of salvation in Christ" but the Scriptures reveal that only those who "believe" are saved. Now let us look at the following verse:

"Wherefore, as by one man sin entered into the world, and death by sin; and so death passed upon all men, for that all have sinned"(Ro.5:12).

Schreiner says that the "death" under discussion is caused by a person's own individual sinning, writing that "*5:12cd teaches that death spread to all because all sinned...Paul regularly argues in Romans 5 and 6 that sin begets death, context supports the interpretation, 'and so death spread to all men because all sinned'...to paraphrase: 'death spread to all people because all sinned individually.'* " [29]

Douglas J. Moo, another defender of the theory of Original Sin, writes that "*Paul certainly uses the verb 'sin' regularly to denote voluntary sinful acts committed by individuals; and this is what most commentators think that this same word, in the same tense as is used here (aorist), designates in 3:23: that all people, 'in their own persons,' commit sins. Probably a majority of contemporary scholars interpret 5:12d, then, to assert that the death of each person (v.12c) is directly caused by that person's own individual sinning.*" [30]

A majority of contemporary scholars agree that the "death" spoken of by Paul at Romans 5:12c is directly caused by the sins which individuals commit.

Personal Sins Result in Spiritual Death

The following passage speaks of individual sins and the results which follow:

"*Behold, the LORD's hand is not shortened, that it cannot save; neither his ear heavy, that it cannot hear. But your iniquities have separated between you and your God, and your sins have hid his face from you, that he will not hear. For your hands are defiled with blood, and your fingers with iniquity; your lips have spoken lies, your tongue hath muttered perverseness*" (Isa.59:1-3).

From this we know that when a person sins that sin separates him from God. Schreiner understands that this separation is referring to spiritual death:

"*Both Adam and Eve when they sinned died spiritually in that they were separated from God.*" [31]

In his comments on the "death" mentioned at Romans 5:12, Moo wrote the following:

"*But what does Paul mean by death here? He may refer*

to physical death only, since 'death' in verse 14 seems to have this meaning. But the passsage goes on to contrast death with eternal life (v. 21). Moreover, in verses 16 and 18 Paul uses 'condemnation' in the same way that he uses 'death' here. These points suggest that Paul is referring to 'spiritual' death: the estrangement from God that is a result of sin, and that, if not healed through Christ, will lead to 'eternal' death." [32]

In the first chapter evidence from the Scriptures was given which demonstrates that it is personal sins which result in spiritual death and not the one sin of Adam..

All Died Spiritually So All Were Previously Alive Spiritually

Now let us look at the following verse again:

"Wherefore, as by one man sin entered into the world, and death by sin; and so death passed upon all men, for that all have sinned" (Ro.5:12).

Paul is saying that spiritual death passed upon "all" people because "all" have sinned. That can only mean that at some point in time "all" people are spiritually alive. The word "death" means "end of life" so we can understand that before "all" people die spiritually they were "all" alive spiritually before they sinned. And the only way that "all" people can be spiritually alive is because they all emerge from the womb spiritually alive.

This fact alone proves that the theory of Original Sin is false.

Schreiner's teaching contradicts the simple fact that all people are born in a state which can only be described as being spiritually alive when he writes that *"human beings enter into the world condemned and spiritually dead because of Adam's one sin...human beings do not enter into the world in a neutral state. They are 'dead upon arrival' because of*

Adam's sin." ³³

The Riddle

In his book *Original Sin: Illuminating the Riddle* Henri Blocher writes the following:

"Romans 5:12ff. fully deserves the appellation 'sedes doctrinae,' the 'seat' or 'fundament' of the doctrine of original sin. Whenever this doctrine is discussed, Romans 5 is in the eye of the storm." ³⁴

Rome teaches that "*the transmission of original sin is a mystery that we cannot fully understand*" (CCC # 404).³⁵

Although Blocher characterizes Original Sin as a "riddle" it is actually the following passage which the proponents of the theory of Original Sin fail to understand and so to them it is a riddle:

"For this cause, even as by one man sin entered into the world, and by sin death; and thus death passed upon all men, for that all have sinned: for until law sin was in the world; but sin is not put to account when there is no law; but death reigned from Adam until Moses, even upon those who had not sinned in the likeness of Adam's transgression, who is the figure of him to come" (Ro.5:12-14; DBY).

Blocher says that Paul's explanation about how Adam communicated a sinful bent to his posterity should be expected in this passage but it is not found there:

"It is rather strange that the core idea, or the hinge of the apostle's purpoted logic - that Adam communicated the sinful bent to his posterity - should not be expressed at all in the passage. It 'might' be explicit; undoubtedly, Paul did share the opinion; yet how surprising that he should not include something here, of all places, to make it clear!" ³⁶

Moo writes that Paul said nothing about how the sin of Adam resulted in the death of everyone:

"*Paul says nothing explicitly about 'how' the sin of one man, Adam, has resulted in death for everyone; nor has he made clear the connection between Adam's sin (v. 12a) and the sin of all people (v. 12d).*" [37]

Besides that Moo says that "*Paul in v.12 asserts that all people sin on their own account; and in vv.18-19 he claims that they all die because of Adam's sin. Paul does not resolve these two perspectives; and we do wrong to try to force a resolution that Paul himseslf never made.*" [38]

The advocates of the theory of Original Sin do in fact force a resolution and according to that resolution all people emerge from the womb with a corrupted nature. That idea is contradicted by the fact that all people emerge from the womb spiritually alive. When the riddle is solved we will see that the solution remains consistent with the fact that people are born into this world spiritually alive.

The Clue that Solves the Riddle

In the following passage Paul does tell us exactly how spiritual death came upon all people when they sin and that evidence will be the clue to understanding in what way Adam's sin resulted in the spiritual death of all people when they sin:

"*For this cause, even as by one man sin entered into the world, and by sin death; and thus death passed upon all men, for that all have sinned: for until law sin was in the world; but sin is not put to account when there is no law; but death reigned from Adam until Moses, even upon those who had not sinned in the likeness of Adam's transgression, who is the figure of him to come*" (Ro.5:12-14; DBY).

Paul said that "for" until law sin was in the world; but sin is not put to account when there is no law.

Verse 13 begins with the Greek word *gar* (which is translated 'for') and one of the meanings of that word is "*it adduces the Cause or gives the Reason of a preceding statement or opinion."* [39]

From this we can understand that verses 13-14 will give the clue as to why Paul said that Adam's sin was responsible for bringing death unto all who sin. The "law" referred to at verse 13 can only be the "law" which Paul mentioned earlier in the same epistle and was the only law in effect between Adam and Moses, the law which is written in the heart of which the conscience bears witness:

"For when the Gentiles, which have not the law, do by nature the things contained in the law, these, having not the law, are a law unto themselves: Which shew the work of the law written in their hearts, their conscience also bearing witness" (Ro.2:14-15).

Thomas Schreiner understands that those who lived between Adam and Moses were judged for violating the law inscribed in their hearts:

"Those who lived in the era between Adam and Moses," he says, *"were accountable for their sins, so that they were condemned because they violated God's moral norms. Their sin was counted against them and thus they were judged. Paul himself teaches the same truth in 2:12, when he claims that 'all those who sinned without the law will also perish without the law.'...Gentiles who did not know or possess the Mosaic law were judged for violating the law inscribed on their hearts (2:14-15)...Romans 2:12 is of paramount importance, for it prevents us from adopting a mistaken view of 5:12-14."* [40]

In his commentary on Romans 5:13 we can see that Albert Barnes came to the same conclusion:

"But sin is not imputed - Is not charged against people, or they are not held guilty of it where there is no law. This is a self-evident proposition, for sin is a violation of law; and if

there is no law, there can be no wrong. Assuming this as a self-evident proposition, the connection is, that there must have been a law of some kind; a 'law written on their hearts,' since sin was in the world, and people could not be charged with sin, or treated as sinners, unless there was some law." [41]

From this we can understand that all people who lived between Adam and Eve died spiritually when they sinned against their conscience. And in some way Adam's sin was responsible for all people having a conscience. With this evidence to guide us it is not difficult to solve the riddle.

The Riddle Solved

The solution as to how Adam's sin was responsible for all people dying spiritually when they sinned is found here:

"And the LORD God said, Behold, the man is become as one of us, to know good and evil: and now, lest he put forth his hand, and take also of the tree of life, and eat, and live for ever" (Gen.3:22).

When Adam sinned by eating of the tree of the knowledge of good and evil he received a conscience. And then all of his posterity were made in his image, also having a conscience:

"And Adam lived an hundred and thirty years, and begat a son in his own likeness, and after his image; and called his name Seth" (Gen.5:3).

If Adam would have remained in a state of innocence and had not sinned then he would not have received this consciousness of the law written in his heart and therefore his descendants would not have received this consciousness so any sin they committed would not have been counted against them because "sin is not imputed when there is no law." Therefore, none of them would have died spiritually when they sinned since they would not have had a conscience.

In his comments on these verses John Wesley wrote that after eating of the forbidden tree Adam and Eve received a conscience:

"The Eyes of them both were opened - The eyes of their consciences; their hearts smote them for what they had done. Now, when it was too late, they saw the happiness they were fallen from, and the misery they were fallen into. They saw God provoked, his favour forfeited, his image lost." [42]

Clarence Larkin wrote: *"Adam and Eve had no conscience before the 'Fall.' Conscience is a knowledge of 'Good' and 'Evil,' and this Adam and Eve did not have until they had their eyes opened by eating of the 'Fruit' of the 'Tree of the Knowledge of Good and Evil.'"* [43]

Renald E. Showers writes that *"Genesis 3:5 and 22 indicate that mankind obtained its awareness of good and evil as a result of eating the forbidden fruit. In other words, the human conscience began when man rebelled against God...Paul indicated that the conscience is the awareness of good and evil which exists inside human beings. It condemns people internally when they do something in the category of evil, and it commends them internally when they do something in the category of good."* [44]

We also read the following in *The Popular Encyclopedia of Bible Prophecy*:

"The Edenic covenant is tied to the dispensation of innocence, whereby God tested man to see if he would live by God's conditions. God told man not to eat of the fruit of the tree of the knowledge of good and evil (Genesis 2:17). The dispensation ended in man's failure--Eve was deceived (1 Timothy 2:14) and Adam deliberately disobeyed. As a result, the first man had personal and experiental knowledge of

good and evil. What seemed like a simple, limited act of eating fruit ended in a broad, conscious knowledge of right and wrong. In the next dispensation, the descendants of Adam were responsible for this new awareness of sin." [45]

Again, if Adam would have obeyed the LORD then he would have remained in a state of "innocence" so therefore "law" would not have come upon his descendants: *"when there is no law, sin is not imputed."* This principle is explained in the following verse:

"Therefore to him that knoweth to do good, and doeth it not, to him it is sin" (Jas.4:17).

God will not impute sin into a person's account unless that person first knows the difference between what is good and what is not.

Therefore we can understand that if the people who lived between the time of Adam until Moses had no inborn knowledge of what is good and what is evil then sin would not have been imputed into their accounts because *"when there is no law sin is not imputed."* And since Adam was responsible for all people having a conscience then in an indirect way Adam's sin lead to the spiritual death of all men because all men die spiritually as a result of their own sin against their conscience.

Romans 5:15

Next, we will see that the verses which follow give even more evidence that the theory of Original Sin is contradicted by the Scriptures.

"But not as the offence, so also is the free gift. For if through the offence of one many be dead, much more the grace of God, and the gift by grace, which is by one man, Jesus Christ, hath abounded unto many" (Ro.5:15).

Here we read that because of the offence of Adam

"many" died but not "all." This verse alone refutes the teaching of Original Sin because according to those who promote the idea of Original Sin "all" people emerge from the womb spiritually dead. In this verse the Greek word translated "many" is used twice and the second time it is used it is impossible that the reference is to "all":

"But not as the offence, so also is the free gift. For if through the offence of one many be dead, much more the grace of God, and the gift by grace, which is by one man, Jesus Christ, hath abounded unto many" (Ro.5:15).

It is a fact that the second time the word "many" is used it cannot possibly be referring to "all" because the gift by grace has not abounded unto "all." Only those with faith receive the gift and not all people have faith. In the passage starting at verse 15 until verse 19 we see Paul employ a figure of speech called Parallelism:

"Parallelism ; or, Parallel Lines. The repetition of similiar, synonymous, or opposite thoughts or words in parallel or successive lines." [46]

John Murray recognized this same literary device, writing that *"Adam is the type of the one to come (v. 14). Adam as the one is parallel to Jesus Christ as the one (v. 17). The one trespass unto condemnation is parallel to the one righteousness unto justification (v. 18). The disobedience of the one is parallel to the obedience of one (v.18)."* [47]

In order to be logically consistent in regard to this parallelism the Greek word translated "many" cannot have one meaning the first time it is used and then have an entirely different meaning the second time it is used. Therefore, it is impossible that Paul is saying that as a result of Adam's sin "all" have died spiritually.

The reason why Paul says that "many" die and not "all" is because it is only those who sin who experience spiritual death--"*and thus death passed upon all men, for that all have sinned*" (Ro.5:12; DBY).

Since children have not sinned they have not died spiritually so that is why Paul says that this death passed unto "many" and not "all." The following verse gives more evidence to support this truth:

"*Moreover your little ones, which ye said should be a prey, and your children, which in that day had no knowledge between good and evil, they shall go in thither, and unto them will I give it, and they shall possess it*" (Deut.1:39).

Jack S.Deere writes that "*God seems to acknowledge a so-called 'age of accountability' for children. Apparently children are not held accountable by God until they are aware of the difference between good and bad.*" [48]

Children are not held responsible for any sin until they can tell the difference between good and evil:

"*Therefore to him that knoweth to do good, and doeth it not, to him it is sin*" (Jas.4:17).

Therefore, we can understand that since little children do not sin and do not experience spiritual death then that explains why Paul said that "many" but not "all" experience spiritual death.

According to the theory of Original Sin "all" people emerge from the womb spiritually dead so Schreiner says that in this verse "many" means "all":

"*The word 'many' here certainly means 'all,' as subsequent verses attest. No room is allowed for exceptions. All of humanity, apart from Christ, died because Adam sinned.*" [49]

Rome also asserts that the word "many means "all," writing the following: "*"By one man's disobedience many (that is, all men) were made sinners*" (CCC # 42).[50]

Now we will address the verses which Schreiner asserts that all people die spiritually as a result of Adam's sin.

Romans 5:18

"*Therefore as by the offence of one judgment came upon all men to condemnation; even so by the righteousness of one the free gift came upon all men unto justification of life*" (Ro.5:18; KJV).

A better translation is found here:

"*so then as it was by one offence towards all men to condemnation, so by one righteousness towards all men for justification of life*" (Romans 5:18; DBY).

John Witmer wrote that "*The provision in the one righteous act, therefore, is potential and it comes to the entire human race as the offer and opportunity which are applied only to 'those who receive' (v. 17)*" [51]

Here is the offer and opportunity which appeared to all people: "*For the grace of God that bringeth salvation hath appeared to all men*" (Titus 2:11). The grace of God that brings salvation is the gospel of grace and the LORD's intent is that all people should believe that gospel which results in the free gift unto justification of life but not all believe the gospel.

In his comments on Romans 5:18 Sir Robert Anderson wrote, "*As by one act of sin judgment came unto all men to condemnation, even so through one act of righteousness the free gift came unto men to justification of life.' Not that all men are in fact made righteous--that is for the many, not for all--but that such was the direction and tendency of the grace*" [52]

In his comments on verse 18 John Nelson Darby differentiates between the intention (scope) of the action from its actual application: "*In Verse 18 the general argument is resumed in a very abstract way. 'By one offence,' he says, 'towards all for condemnation, even so by one accomplished righteousness (or act of righteousness) towards all men, for justification of life. One offence bore in its bearing, so to speak, referred to all, and so it was with the one act of righteousness. This is the scope of the action in itself. Now for the application: for as by the disobedience of one man (only) many are constituted sinners, so by the obedience of one (only) many are constituted righteous."* **53**

The "scope" of the one offense towards all people to condemnation is that all people will be condemned and die spiritually when they sin against their consciences. But since infants and young children do not yet have a fully developed conscience they are not held accountable until they are aware of the difference between good and bad. So Darby was correct when he wrote, "*or as by the disobedience of one man (only) many are constituted sinners.*"

This demonstrates that Schreiner was in error when he asserted that Romans 5:18 teaches that "all" people are condemned as a result of the sin of Adam.

Romans 5:19

"*For as by one man's disobedience many were made sinners, so by the obedience of one shall many be made righteous*" (Ro.5:19).

Here we read that "many" will be made righteous. And since not "all" people will be made righteous then it is impossible that the word "many" refers to all people. Five times Paul contrasts Adam with the Lord Jesus at Romans 5:15-19 and the sustained parallelism in these verses forbids the idea that when the word "many" is used in the first instance it means "all" and the second time it is used it doesn't mean "all" but instead only "many."

Romans 5:20-21

"Moreover the law entered, that the offence might abound. But where sin abounded, grace did much more abound: That as sin hath reigned unto death, even so might grace reign through righteousness unto eternal life by Jesus Christ our Lord" (Ro.5:20-21).

Previously Paul had been speaking of the law written in the heart of all men of which the conscience bears witness. But now he speaks of the Law given by Moses and he says that law "entered that the offense might abound" or increase. How did the giving of the law result in the offense increasing?

The law written in the heart of every person is limited in some respects because it does not reveal all of the LORD's demands for personal righteousness. In the following verse Paul says that he wouldn't have known that coveting is a sin unless he had been given the following commandment found in the Law of Moses:

"What shall we say then? Is the law sin? God forbid. Nay, I had not known sin, but by the law: for I had not known lust, except the law had said, Thou shalt not covet" (Ro.7:7).

Physical Death and Spiritual Death?

Schreiner says that the words "eternal life" found in verse 21 indicate that the death cannot be restricted to physical death because it must also be in regard to "spiritual death: *"The death introduced by Adam is conjoined with 'condemnation' (vv.16, 18), and it is also contrasted with 'eternal life' (v.21). Thus it can hardly be restricted to physical death...I am not suggesting that physical death and spiritual death can ultimately be separated, for the former is the culmination and outworking of the latter."* [54]

Even though Schreiner asserts that physical death and spiritual death cannot be separated the facts say otherwise. People die spiritually when they sin but people die physically because they have been denied the very thing which would allow them to live forever in their physical bodies--the Tree of Life:

"And the LORD God said, Behold, the man is become as one of us, to know good and evil: and now, lest he put forth his hand, and take also of the tree of life, and eat, and live for ever: Therefore the LORD God sent him forth from the garden of Eden, to till the ground from whence he was taken. So he drove out the man; and he placed at the east of the garden of Eden Cherubims, and a flaming sword which turned every way, to keep the way of the tree of life" (Gen.3:22-25).

From this we can see that in order for Adam to live forever it was necessary for him to eat of the Tree of Life. And the same can be said of all of his posterity. Since the way to the Tree of Life has been denied to all of Adam's descendants then people die physically because they cannot eat of that tree. As a result of that people die physically:

"And as it is appointed unto men once to die, but after this the judgment" (Heb.9:27).

Therefore, the "death" spoken of in the following verse can only be referring to spiritual death:

"Wherefore, as by one man sin entered into the world, and death by sin; and so death passed upon all men, for that all have sinned" (Ro.5:12).

Since all people die spiritually when they sin then all people must have first been alive spiritually before they sinned. And the only way that could possibly happen is because all people emerge from the womb spiritually alive.

That fact alone proves that the theory of Original Sin cannot possibly be correct.

Returning to the subject of infant baptism Sir Robert

Anderson writes the following about what he calls the "*gross and profane misrepresentation of God*" which "*is an essential part of the historic religion of Christendom*":

"*HERE is an infant, born but yesterday, and yet so frail and sickly that its young life may flicker out at any moment. The question arises, If it should die, what is to be its future? If it dies in its present condition, we are told it must be lost, heaven it cannot enter. But, we plead, the poor creature does not know its right hand from its left ; it is absolutely innocent. Why should it be thus punished? Personally innocent, yes, we are answered; but by natural generation it belongs to the fallen race, and Adam's sin must banish it to hell, unless by regeneration it is brought within the family of God. But by the sacrament of baptism this change can be brought about without delay or difficulty, and thus the child's salvation can be secured if death should seize on it. Any one, perhaps, can perform the rite; but, as that is a disputed point, it may be well to make assurance still more sure, and call in the aid of one who is divinely appointed to administer the sacraments. But suppose the man we summon to our aid should be false to his profession, and prove to be of evil character and immoral life?*

"*That, we are assured, will in no way affect the validity of the sacrament, or the reality of the change which it will produce in the child. If the man be lawfully ordained, God will acknowledge him as His minister, notwithstanding.*

"*In a case of this kind nothing is gained by an appeal to passion. But will thoughtful and fair minds consider the matter, and honestly answer the question, whether even in the superstitions of Pagan races to whom we send out missionaries, there can be found a conception of God more unworthy, more revolting than this.*

"*What kind of God is this that is thus presented to us? A Being, unjust, unloving, and cruel, who devotes an innocent and helpless infant to destruction. A Being, unreasonable, arbitrary, and capricious, who will change its eternal destiny if a few drops of water are sprinkled upon it, accompanied by the utterance of a few cabalistic words. An unholy, an immoral Being, for He employs and recognises agents no matter what their character and life may be."* [55]

End Notes

1. *The Catechism of the Catholic Church,* Part Two, Section Two, Chapter One, Article 1: The Sacrament of Baptism.

2. *The Catechism of the Catholic Church*, Part One, Section Two, Chapter One, Article 1:, Paragraph 7. The Fall.

3. *Ibid.*

4. Thomas R. Schreiner, "Original Sin and Original Death," in *Adam, The Fall, and Original sin* ed. Hans Madueme and Michael Reeves (Grand Rapids: Baker Academic, 2014), 276.

.5. *The Catechism of the Catholic Church*, Part One, Section Two, Chapter One, Article 1:, Paragraph 7. The Fall.

6. Matthew Poole, *Matthew Poole's Commentary*; Accessed June 17, 2020, http://biblehub.com/commentaries/poole/hebrews/2.htm.

7. Albert Barnes, *Notes on the Bible by Albert Barnes*; Accessed June 17, 2020, http://biblehub.com/commentaries/barnes/hebrews/2.htm.

8. Mark Dunagan, *Commentaries on the Bible*, "Commentary on Ecclesiastes 7:29; Accessed June 17, 2020, https://www.studylight.org/commentaries/dun/ecclesiastes-7.html.

9. Adam Clarke, *The Adam Clarke Commentary,*; Accessed June 17, 2020, https://www.studylight.org/commentaries/acc/ecclesiastes-7.html.

10. Adam Clarke, *Commentary on the Bible*, Accessed June 17, 2020, https://biblehub.com/commentaries/clarke/1_corinthians/11.htm

11. Henry Morris, *Defender's Study Bible*; Accessed September 8,2018, http://www.icr.org/books/defenders/8530/

12. G.F. Wiggers, An Historical Presentation of Augustinism and Pelagianism From the Original Sources (Andover, MA: Gould, Newman & Saxton, 1840), 97.

13. Joseph Henry Thayer, *A Greek - English Lexicon of the New Testament* (Grand Rapids: Baker Book House, 1977), 474.

14. *Ibid.,* 475.

15. Walter Bauer, *A Greek-English Lexicon of the New Testament and Other Early Christian Literature*, 3rd ed., ed. Frederick William Danker (Chicago: University of Chicago Press, 2000), 752.

16. Joseph Henry Thayer, *A Greek - English Lexicon of the New Testament*, 112.

17. John A. Witmer, "Romans," in *The Bible Knowledge Commentary; New Testament,* ed. John F. Walvoord and Roy B. Zuck (Colorado Springs: Chariot Victor Publishing, 1983), 467.

18. Thomas R. Schreiner, *Adam, the Fall, and Original Sin*, 271.

19. *The Catechism of the Catholic Church,* Part Two, Section Two, Chapter One, Article 1: The Sacrament of Baptism.

20. *The Scofield Study Bible; King James Version* (New York: Oxford University Press, 2003), 1557.

21. *The Pulpit Commentary*, Accessed June 17, 2020, http://biblehub.com/commentaries/pulpit/ephesians/2.htm

22. R.C. Sproul, *What is Reformed Theology?* (Grand Rapids: Baker Books, 1997), 129.

23. *The Expositor's Greek Testament*, ed. W. Robertson

Nicoll, volume III, (New York and London: Hodder and Stoughton), 283.

24. Marvin R. Vincent, *Vincent's Word Studies*; Accessed June 17, 2020, http://biblehub.com/commentaries/vws/colossians/2.htm

25. Joseph Benson, *Benson Commentary on the Old and New Testaments*; Accessed June 17, 2020, https://biblehub.com/commentaries/benson/john/11.htm

26. *The Catechism of the Catholic Church*, Part One, Section Two, Chapter One, Article 1:, Paragraph 7. The Fall.

27. Thomas R. Schreiner, *Adam, the Fall, and Original Sin*, 271.

28. *Catechism of the Catholic Church,* Part One, Section Two, Chapter One, Article I, Paragraph 7.

29. Thomas R. Schreiner, *Adam, the Fall, and Original Sin*, 274, 280.

30. Douglas J. Moo, "Sin in Paul," in *Fallen: A Theology of Sin*, ed. Christoper W. Morgan and Robert A. Peterson (Wheaton IL: Crossway, 2013), 122-3.

31. Thomas R. Schreiner, *Adam, the Fall, and Original Sin*, 272.

32. Douglas Moo, *Fallen: A Theology of Sin*, 121.

33. Thomas R. Schreiner, *Adam, the Fall, and Original Sin*, 283.

34. Henri Blocher, *Original Sin: Illuminating the Riddle* (Downers Grove, IL: InterVarsity Press, 1997), 63.

35. *Catechism of the Catholic Church,* Part One, Section Two, Chapter One, Article I, Paragraph 7.

36. Henri Blocher, *Original Sin: Illuminating the Riddle*, 66.

37. Douglas J. Moo, *Fallen: A Theology of Sin*, 122.

38. Douglas J. Moo, *The Epistle to the Romans* (Grand Rapids: William B. Eerdmans Publishing Co., 1996), 324.

39. John Henry Thayer, *A Greek-English Lexicon of the New Testament* (Grand Rapids: Baker Book House, 1977), 109.

40. Thomas R. Schreiner, *Adam, the Fall and Original Sin*, 279-280.

41. Albert Barnes, *Notes on the Bible*, Commentary on Romans 5; Accessed June 18, 2020, http://www.sacred-texts.com/bib/cmt/barnes/rom005.htm

42. John Wesley, *John Wesley's notes on the Bible*; Accessed June 18, 2020, https://www.biblestudytools.com/commentaries/wesleys-explanatory-notes/genesis/genesis-3.html

43. Clarence Larkin, *Rightly Dividing The Word* [Rev. Clarence Larkin Est.], 19.

44. Renald E. Showers, *The Second Dispensation*, Ankerberg Theological Research Institute; Accessed June 18, 2020, https://www.jashow.org/articles/general/dispensational-theology-part-3/

45. *The Popular Encyclopedia of Bible Prophecy*, ed.Tim LaHaye & Ed Hindson, (Eugene: Harvest House, 2004), 86.

46. *The Companion Bible; King James Version* (Grand Rapids: Kregel Publications, 1990), Appendix 6: Figures of Speech, 11.

47. John Murray, *The Imputation of Adam's Sin* (Phillipsburg, NJ: Presbyterian and Reformed Publishing Co., 1959), 33.

48. Jack S. Deere, "Deuteronomy" in *The Bible Knowledge Commentary; Old Testament* (Colorado Springs: ChariotVictor Publishing, 1985), 264-65.

49. Thomas R. Schreiner, *Adam, the Fall, and Original Sin*, 282.

50. *Catechism of the Catholic Church,* Part One, Section Two, Chapter One, Article I, Paragraph 7.

51. John A. Witmer, "Romans," in *The Bible Knowledge Commentary; New Testament* (Colorado Springs, CO: ChariotVictor Publishing, 1983), 460.

52. Sir Robert Anderson, *The Gospel And Its Ministry* [London: James Nisbet & Co., 1886), 131.

53. John Nelson Darby, *Darby's Synopsis of the Bible*; Accessed August 28, 2018, http://biblehub.com/commentaries/darby/romans/5.htm

54. Thomas R. Schreiner, *Romans*, (Grand Rapids: Baker Academic, 1998), 272.

55. Sir Robert Anderson, *The Bible or the Church?*, 110-111.

Chapter IX. The Popes and Priests of Rome

The Keys to the Kingdom of Heaven

Rome teaches that "*Jesus entrusted a specific authority to Peter: 'I will give you the keys of the kingdom of heaven, and whatever you bind on earth shall be bound in heaven, and whatever you loose on earth shall be loosed in heaven.' The 'power of the keys' designates authority to govern the house of God, which is the Church. Jesus, the Good Shepherd, confirmed this mandate after his Resurrection: 'Feed my sheep.' The power to 'bind and loose' connotes the authority to absolve sins, to pronounce doctrinal judgements, and to make disciplinary decisions in the Church. Jesus entrusted this authority to the Church through the ministry of the apostles and in particular through the ministry of Peter, the only one to whom he specifically entrusted the keys of the kingdom*" (CCC # 553).[1]

According to Rome the 'power of the keys of the kingdom of heaven' designates authority to govern the house of God, which is the Church. However, the "kingdom of heaven" is not the church and the bringing in of the kingdom of heaven remains in the future. John the Baptist preached, "*Repent ye: for the kingdom of heaven is at hand*" (Mt.3:2).

Louis A. Barbieri, Jr., wrote: "*What was John preaching? He announced a coming kingdom, which simply means 'a coming rule.' This rule was to be heaven's rule: 'the kingdom of heaven.' Does this mean God would then began to rule in heavenly spheres? Obiously not, for God has always ruled over heavenly spheres since Creation. John must mean that God's heavenly rule was about to be extended directly to to earthly spheres.*"[2]

Albert Barnes said practically the same thing as Barbieri,

writing that "*The expression 'the kingdom of heaven is at hand' would be best translated, 'the reign of God draws near.' We do not say commonly of a kingdom that it is movable, or that it approaches. A reign may be said to be at hand; and it may be said with propriety that the time when Christ would reign was at hand. In this sense it is meant that the time when Christ should reign, or set up his kingdom, or begin his dominion on earth.*" [3]

The expression the "kingdom of heaven is at hand" refers to the time when Christ should set up his kingdom to begin The Lord Jesus' dominion on earth.

Sir Robert Anderson asked, "*what ground is there for supposing that the Apostle Peter was entrusted with the keys of the Church? The only ground is the fact that to him were given 'the keys of the kingdom of heaven,' and the Church which proudly boasts of being the keeper of Holy Writ is so ignorant of Scripture that it confounds 'the kingdom of heaven' with the Church!*" [4]

Besides that, due to the fact that Israel rejected the Lord Jesus as her promised Messiah the kingdom was postponed until the King returns to the earth. He said:

"*And then shall they see the Son of man coming in a cloud with power and great glory. And when these things begin to come to pass, then look up, and lift up your heads; for your redemption draweth nigh. And he spake to them a parable; Behold the fig tree, and all the trees; When they now shoot forth, ye see and know of your own selves that summer is now nigh at hand. So likewise ye, when ye see these things come to pass, know ye that the kingdom of God is nigh at hand*" (Lk.21:27-31).

According to the Lord Jesus it will no be until He is seen coming in a cloud that the kingdom will be "nigh at hand." It will not be until the kingdom is brought to earth when the Apostles are given the keys to the kingdom of heaven and will "bind on earth" what "shall be bound in heaven." That will not happen until the Apostles will sit upon twelve tribes judging the twelve tribes of Israel in the kingdom:

"That ye may eat and drink at my table in my kingdom, and sit on thrones judging the twelve tribes of Israel" (Lk.22:30).

"And Jesus said unto them, Verily I say unto you, That ye which have followed me, in the regeneration when the Son of man shall sit in the throne of his glory, ye also shall sit upon twelve thrones, judging the twelve tribes of Israel" (Mt.19:28).

This speaks of the millennial reign of the Lord Jesus, the time when Israel will be restored to her previous position of being a special people unto the Lord. Therefore the "keys of the kingdom of heaven" have nothing to do with what is happening now within the Body of Christ.

Upon This Rock I Will Build My Church

Rome teaches the following about the "rock" on which the Lord Jesus will build His church:

"Simon Peter holds the first place in the college of the Twelve; Jesus entrusted a unique mission to him. Through a revelation from the Father, Peter had confessed: 'You are the Christ, the Son of the living God.' Our Lord then declared to him: 'You are Peter, and on this rock I will build my Church, and the gates of Hades will not prevail against it.' Christ, the "living Stone", thus assures his Church, built on Peter, of victory over the powers of death. Because of the faith he confessed Peter will remain the unshakable rock of the Church. His mission will be to keep this faith from every lapse and to strengthen his brothers in it." [5]

Let us look at the following question asked by the Lord Jesus and the answer given by Peter:

"He saith unto them, But whom say ye that I am? And Simon Peter answered and said, Thou art the Christ, the Son of the living God. And Jesus answered and said unto him, Blessed art thou, Simon Barjona: for flesh and blood hath not revealed it unto thee, but my Father which is in heaven. And I say also unto thee, That thou art Peter, and upon this rock I will build my church; and the gates of hell shall not prevail against it" (Mt.16:15-18).

This confession of Peter, that the Lord Jesus is the Christ, the Son of God, is the "rock" upon which the Jewish church was to be built. Chrysostom wrote: "*therefore He added this, And I say unto you, You are Peter, and upon this rock will I build my Church; that is, on the faith of his confession.*" [6]

Alfred Edersheim agrees with Chrysostom, and he explains the meaning of the "rock" here:

"*Perhaps it might be expressed in this somewhat clumsy paraphrase: 'Thou art Peter (Petros)--a Stone or Rock--and upon this Petra--the Rock, the Petrine--will I found My Church...so Christ promised that He would build His Church on the Petrine in Peter--on his faith and confession.*" [7]

Next, it will be demonstrated that when the Lord Jesus said "*Upon this rock I will build my church,*" the church to which He made reference is not the Church, which is His body.

Tell It To The Church (*Ekklesia*)

Let us look at the following words of the Lord Jesus where He speaks of the church (*Ekklesia*):

"*Moreover if thy brother shall trespass against thee, go and tell him his fault between thee and him alone: if he shall hear thee, thou hast gained thy brother. But if he will not hear thee, then take with thee one or two more, that in the mouth of two or three witnesses every word may be established. And if he shall neglect to hear them, tell it unto the church (ekklesia): but if he neglect to hear the church, let him be unto thee as an heathen man and a publican. Verily I say unto you, Whatsoever ye shall bind on earth shall be bound in heaven: and whatsoever ye shall loose on earth shall be loosed in heaven"*(Mt.18:15-18).

In his commentary on this passage Acts 2 Louis A. Barbieri, Jr., writes: "*two or three witnesses should be taken along for a clear testimony. This was in keeping with Old Testament precedents, as in Deuteronomy 19:15. If the sinning brother still failed to recognize his error, the situation should be told before the entire church, or 'assembly.' The disciples probably would have understood Jesus to mean the matter should be brought before the Jewish assembly.*" [8]

In the *Cambridge Bible for Schools and Colleges* we read that the word church in this passage means "*either (1) the assembly or congregation of the Jewish synagogue, or rather, (2) the ruling body of the synagogue (collegium presbyterorum, Schleusner) is meant. This must have been the sense of the word to those who were listening to Christ.*" [9]

The Birth of the Church (Ekklesia)

Pope John Paul II said that "*the Second Vatican Council speaks of the Church's birth on the day of Pentecost.*" [10]

According to Rome the Church, which is the Body of Christ, began on the day of Pentecost. Let us look at the following verse which speaks of the "church" on the day of Pentecost:

"*Praising God, and having favour with all the people. And the Lord added to the church (ekklesia) daily such as should be saved*" (Acts 2:47).

The Greek word translated "church" is *ekklesia* and that word can be found in the Greek version of the Old Testament (the *LXX*). Joseph Henry Thayer says that one of the meanings of that word as found in the LXX is "*the assembly of Israelites...esp. when gathered for sacred purposes.*" [11]

Alfred Edersheim wrote the following:

"*Nor would the term 'Church' sound strange in Jewish ears. The same Greek word (ekklesia), as the equivalent of the Hebrew 'Qahal,' 'convocation,' 'the called,' occurs in the LXX. rendering of the Old Testament, and in 'the Wisdom of the Son of Sirach' and was apparently in familiar use at that time. In Hebrew use it referred to Israel, not in their national but in their religious unity.*" [12]

According to Edersheim the Greek word translated "church" was in familiar use and "*it referred to Israel...in their religious unity.*".

The word *ekklesia* is translated "congregation" in the following passage found in the Greek Old Testamemt (LXX) and the context reveals that it is Israel and only Israel which is in view:

"*Sound the trumpet in Sion, sanctify a fast, proclaim a [solemn] service: gather the people, sanctify the congregation (ekklesia), assemble the elders, gather the infants at the breast: let the bridegroom go forth of his chamber, and the bride out of her closet...And it shall come to pass afterward, that I will pour out of my Spirit upon all flesh; and your sons and your daughters shall prophesy, and your old men shall dream dreams, and your young men shall see visions*" (Joel 2:15-16, 3:1; LXX).

This passage is speaking about the religious unity of Israel's congregation (*ekklesia*) and it foretells of the LORD pouring out His spirit and that the Israelites will prophesy. And that is exactly what Peter said was happening (this is that) on the day of Pentecost:

"*For these are not drunken, as ye suppose, seeing it is but the third hour of the day. But this is that which was spoken by the prophet Joel; And it shall come to pass in the last days, saith God, I will pour out of my Spirit upon all flesh: and your sons and your daughters shall prophesy, and your young men shall see visions, and your old men shall dream dreams"* (Acts 2:16-17).

Therefore, it is clear that the *ekklesia* at Acts 2 is in regard to the congregation (*ekklesia*) of Israel in her religious unity. The word *ekklesia* at Acts 2 does not refer to the Church, which is His Body (Eph.1:22-23).

Peter's Second Pentecostal Sermon

Here is what Peter said in his second Pentecostal sermon:

"Repent ye therefore, and be converted, that your sins may be blotted out, that the times of refreshing shall come from the presence of the Lord; And he shall send Jesus Christ, which before was preached unto you: Whom the heaven must receive until the times of restitution of all things, which God hath spoken by the mouth of all his holy prophets since the world began" (Acts 3:19-21).

Sir Robert Anderson wrote the following commentary on Peter's words at Acts 3:19-21:

"To represent this as Christian doctrine, or the institution of 'a new religion,' is to betray ignorance alike of Judaism and of Christianity. The speakers were Jews--the apostles of One who was Himself 'a minister of the circumcision.' Their hearers were Jews, and as Jews they were addressed. The Pentecostal Church which was based upon the testimony was intensely and altogether Jewish. It was not merely that the converts were Jews, and none but Jews, but that the idea of evangelising Gentiles never was even mooted. When the first great persecution scattered the disciples, and they 'went everywhere preaching the Word,' they preached, we are expressly told, 'to none but to the Jews' (Acts xi. 19)." [13]

Because Peter was commanding the nation of Israel to

repent and since he had received the Holy Spirit to guide him in all truth (Jn.16:13) then it is certain that the LORD's purpose on that day was in regard to the nation of Israel and not to the Body of Christ.

Stanley Toussaint understands that at Acts 3 the LORD was dealing with the nation of Israel and not the Church, which is His Body:

"Was Peter saying here that if Israel repented, God's kingdom would have come to earth? This must be answered in the affirmative...Acts 3:17-21 shows that Israel's repentance was to have had two purposes: (1) for 'individual' Israelites there was a forgiveness of sins, and (2) for 'Israel as a nation' her Messiah would return to reign." [14]

Arno C. Gaebelein also understands that Peter was addressing the nation of Israel, writing the following: *"Peter delivers his second address. Interesting and of much importance are Acts 3:19-21. They can only be understood in the right way if we do not lose sight of the fact to whom they were addressed, that is to Jews, and not to Gentiles. They are the heart of this discourse, and as such a God-given appeal and promise to the nation."* [15]

The first thing which needs to be understood in determining the beginning of the Body of Christ is that the LORD's program for Israel is distinct from His program for the Body of Christ. The Scriptures reveal that circumcision was a requirement for the sons of Israel and any uncirumcised male was cut off from the nation of Israel:

"This is my covenant, which ye shall keep, between me and you and thy seed after thee; Every man child among you shall be circumcised. And ye shall circumcise the flesh of your foreskin; and it shall be a token of the covenant betwixt me and you...And the uncircumcised man child whose flesh of his foreskin is not circumcised, that soul shall be cut off from his people; he hath broken my covenant" (Gen.17:10-

11,14).

However, circumcision profits no one during the Church age, as witnessed by Paul's words here:

"For in Jesus Christ neither circumcision availeth any thing, nor uncircumcision; but faith which worketh by love" (Gal.5:6).

The Scriptures also reveal that when the nation of Israel was in a covenant relationship with the LORD the children of Israel were a special people unto Him above all people upon the face of the earth:

"For thou art an holy people unto the LORD thy God: the LORD thy God hath chosen thee to be a special people unto himself, above all people that are upon the face of the earth" (Deut.7:6).

On the other hand, during the Church age there are no special people unto the LORD except for believers and in the Body of Christ there is no distinction between the Jews and those of other nationalities:

"And have put on the new man, which is renewed in knowledge after the image of him that created him: Where there is neither Greek nor Jew, circumcision nor uncircumcision, Barbarian, Scythian, bond nor free: but Christ is all, and in all" (Col.3:10-11).

In his comments on these verses Norman L. Geisler writes the following:

"In Christ distinctions are removed. These include national distinctions (Greek or Jew...); religious distinctions (circumcised or uncircumcised)..." [16]

These facts serve to prove that when the LORD's program for Israel is in view then that program cannot be about the Body of Christ because His two different programs are mutually exclusive. In other words, when the Divine plan toward Israel is in effect then the children of Israel are above all people on the face of the earth so therefore it is impossible that at the same time the Divine plan is also toward the Body of Christ where there is no difference between the Jews and other nationalities. Sir Robert Anderson wrote the following:

"For just as we aver that 'God cannot lie,' we may assert that He cannot act at the same time upon two wholly different and incompatible principles." [17]

Since Peter was addressing the nation of Israel on the day of Pentecost then it is obvious that he was not addressing those in the Body of Christ so it is impossible that the Body of Christ began on the day of Pentecost.

The Pope Acts in the Place of Christ

According to Rome *"The Pope, visible head of the Church on earth, acting for and in the place of Christ."* [18]

Sir Robert Anderson writes the following about Pope Alexander VI and who in their right mind can imagine that Pope was acting in the place of Christ?:

"When the sixteenth century opened, the infamous Alexander VI. was on the papal throne. The letter of a devout Roman Catholic, recorded in the diary of a high official in personal attendance on the Pope, describes life in the Vatican under the Borgias. Here are extracts from it: 'Everything can be had for money. Crimes grosser than Scythian are committed without disguise under the eyes of the Pope. There are rapes, murders, incests, debaucheries, cruelties, exceeding those of the Neros and Caligulas. Licentiousness past description is paraded in contempt of God and man. Sons and daughters are polluted. Harlots and procuresses are gathered together in the mansion of St. Peter. On All Saints' day fifty women of the town were invited to dinner.' At this point the historian from whom the foregoing

is quoted breaks off the narrative by adding: 'The details of what followed are barely mentionable.' The letter goes on to speak of the universal sale of indulgences, to provide a portion for the Pope's daughter, Lucretia, and also to mention his son Cesar Borgia as being as great a monster as himself. And as for the Sacred College, not a single voice is raised in warning or remonstrance. Was it any wonder that when Charles V. ascended the Imperial throne the laity everywhere were in revolt against the Church?" [19]

Pope Pius XII and Adolf Hitler

On the first of May 1938, the 'Mercare de France,' a French magazine, reminded us what that magazine had said four years previously:

"The 'Mercure de France of the 15th of January 1934 said--and no one contradicted it--that it was Pope Pius XII who 'made' Hitler. He came to power, not so much through legal means, but because the pope influenced the Centrum (german catholic party)." [20]

In an article titled "Hitler's Pope" we read the following: *"Long-buried Vatican files reveal a new and shocking indictment of World War II's Pope Pius XII: that in pursuit of absolute power he helped Adolf Hitler destroy German Catholic political opposition, betrayed the Jews of Europe, and sealed a deeply cynical pact with a 20th-century devil. "* [21]

We also know that Pope Pius XII did his best to keep secret the fact that the Nazi's were systematically murdering Jews during the Holocaust:

"Pope Pius XII, the leader of the Roman Catholic Church during World War II, learned about the mass murder of Jews early in the war but kept the information a secret in the Vatican. That was the charge made by a German historian Hubert Wolf, who is also a priest, and a team of scholars he

assembled to study the recently opened archives of the church leader. Wolf confirmed May 16 that scholars found new evidence the Pope misled the United States government about the systematic murder of Jews in Poland and the Ukraine...President Franklin Roosevelt's personal representative to the Vatican, Myron Taylor, pressed the Pope to speak out against Hitler and Nazi atrocities. Throughout the war, the Pope remained silent." [22]

Steven Pressman said, *"What we are dealing with is a pope who did not denounce the Nazis. He was skeptical of taking a strong stance against what the Nazis were doing to the Jews in Europe. He refused to support the allies."* [23]

"Settimia Spizzichino, the sole Roman Jewish woman survivor from the death camps said, 'I came back from Auschwitz on my own. I lost my mother, two sisters, a niece, and one brother. Pius XII could have warned us about what was going to happen. We might have escaped from Rome and joined the partisans. He played right into the Germans' hands. It all happened right under his nose. But he was an anti-Semitic Pope, a pro-German Pope. He didn't take a single risk. And when they say the Pope is like Jesus Christ, it is not true. He did not save a single child. Nothing." [24]

Pope Pius XII "made Hitler" and no one was more responsible for World War II than Hitler. Therefore, Pope Pius XII was responsible for the estimated total of 70-85 million people who perished during that war:

"Without Hitler implementing his genocidal theories, its possible the massacre of millions of Jews and other minorities in the Holocaust would have been averted, even if anti-Semitism itself would still have persisted. Perhaps the Weimar Republic might have avoided Nazi Germany's descent into militarism and authoritarianism." [25]

Pagan Priests

Rome teaches that *"The chosen people was constituted by God as 'a kingdom of priests and a holy nation.' But within the people of Israel, God chose one of the twelve tribes, that of Levi, and set it apart for liturgical service; God himself is its inheritance. A special rite consecrated the beginnings of the priesthood of the Old Covenant. The priests are 'appointed to act on behalf of men in relation to God, to offer gifts and sacrifices for sins"* (CCC # 1539).[26]

Sir Robert Anderson wrote the following about the so-called "priests" of the church at Rome:

"Save in the sense in which every Christian is a priest, there can be no priest on earth apart from the family of Aaron. This rule is so absolute that it applies even to Christ Himself. As the Epistle to the Hebrews emphatically declares, 'If He were on earth He would not be a priest at all.' Therefore if any one claims to be a priest, he must be a Pagan priest." [27]

Presbyterate

Rome lists the three degrees of apostolic ministry:

"Holy Orders is the sacrament through which the mission entrusted by Christ to his apostles continues to be exercised in the Church until the end of time: thus it is the sacrament of apostolic ministry. It includes three degrees: episcopate, presbyterate, and diaconate" (CCC # 1536).[28]

According to *The Catholic Dictionary* the presbterate is *"the priesthood, as the second rank of holy orders above the diaconate and below the episcopate. (Etym. Greek presbyteros, elder.)."* [29]

The Greek word translated "elders" in the following verse is *presbyteros*"

"For this cause left I thee in Crete, that thou shouldest set in order the things that are wanting, and ordain elders

(presbyteros) in every city, as I had appointed thee" (Titus 1:5).

On the other hand, the Greek word translated "priesthood" in the following verse is *hierateia*:

"*And verily they that are of the sons of Levi, who receive the office of the priesthood (hierateia), have a commandment to take tithes of the people according to the law...*" (Heb.7:5).

According to Rome the Greek word *presbyteros* means "priesthood" despite the fact that the Greek word for "priesthood is *hierateia.*

The Sacrament of Penance

According to Rome the "Sacrament of Penance" "*is called the 'sacrament of confession,' since the disclosure or confession of sins to a priest is an essential element of this sacrament.*" (CCC # 1422).[30]

Rome also teaches that "*It is called the 'sacrament of forgiveness,' since by the priest's sacramental absolution God grants the penitent 'pardon and peace.'*" (CCC # 1424).[31]

The Scriptures reveal that believers are to confess their sins "to each other":

"*Therefore confess your sins to each other and pray for each other so that you may be healed*" (Jas.5:16; NIV).

Also, we read this:

"*For if we would judge ourselves, we should not be judged. But when we are judged, we are chastened of the Lord, that we should not be condemned with the world*" (1 Cor.11:31-32).

If a Christian judges himself in regard to his sins then in effect he is confessing his sins to himself. But the Scriptures will be searched in vain where anyone is told to confess his sins to a priest.

The Sacrificing Priests of Rome

According to Rome her common priesthood is in regard to a participation in the "one priesthood of Christ":

"The ministerial or hierarchical priesthood of bishops and priests, and the common priesthood of all the faithful participate, 'each in its own proper way, in the one priesthood of Christ.'" (CCC # 1547).[32]

One of the duties of the priest is to offer sacrifices for sins:

"The chosen people was constituted by God as 'a kingdom of priests and a holy nation.' But within the people of Israel, God chose one of the twelve tribes, that of Levi, and set it apart for liturgical service; God himself is its inheritance. A special rite consecrated the beginnings of the priesthood of the Old Covenant. The priests are "appointed to act on behalf of men in relation to God, to offer gifts and sacrifices for sins" (CCC # 1539).[33]

According to Rome one of the ministries of her priests is to offer sacrifices for sin and that ministry is a participation in the "one priesthood of Christ." However, the Lord Jesus' ministry had nothing to do with offering sacrifices for sins. There are many within Christendom who think that the Lord Jesus officiated as priest at His own death because of what we read here:

"But this man, after he had offered one sacrifice for sins for ever, sat down on the right hand of God" (Heb.10:11-12).

In order to understand this verse a correct understanding of the meaning of the word "offered" is necessary so let us look at how the word is used in the following passage which speaks of sacrifice:

"And the LORD called unto Moses, and spake unto him out of the tabernacle of the congregation, saying, Speak unto the children of Israel, and say unto them, If any man of you bring an offering unto the LORD...let him offer a male without blemish: he shall offer it of his own voluntary will at the door of the tabernacle of the congregation before the LORD" (Lev.1:1-3).

The Jews offered or presented his sacrifice at the door of the tabernacle. Sir Robert Anderson wrote the following about this subject:

"This ritual will enable us to understand those wonderful words already quoted, that Christ 'offered Himself without spot to God.' This was not at the Cross, but when, 'on coming into the world,' He said, 'Lo, I come to do Thy will, O God' (Heb.x. 5,7). As the result, the divine will led Him to His death of shame. But neither His death, nor the self-surrender which led to His death, was a part of His High-priestly work." [34]

In fact, when the Lord Jesus walked the earth He was not a priest so when He died at the Cross it was impossible that He was acting in His role as High Priest:

"For if he were on earth, he should not be a priest, seeing that there are priests that offer gifts according to the law" (Heb.8:4).

Anderson wrote, *"Christ is both Mediator and Priest. And His priesthood is of the order of Meichisedek (Heb. vii. 15-16), whose ministry was not to sacrifice for sins, but to succour and bless. It began therefore, not with Calvary, but with His ascension to the right hand of God."* [35]

Despite these facts Rome teaches that the sacrifice of Christ which is in the Eucharist (the unbloody sacrifice) is completed by the ministry of the priests:

"Through the ministry of priests the spiritual sacrifice of

the faithful is completed in union with the sacrifice of Christ the only Mediator, which in the Eucharist is offered through the priests' hands in the name of the whole Church in an unbloody and sacramental manner until the Lord himself comes" (CCC # 1369).[36]

Forbidding to Marry

According the Rome their priests are to live a celibate life so therefore they are not to marry:

"*All the ordained ministers of the Latin Church, with the exception of permanent deacons, are normally chosen from among men of faith who live a celibate life and who intend to remain celibate 'for the sake of the kingdom of heaven.' Called to consecrate themselves with undivided heart to the Lord and to "the affairs of the Lord, 'they give themselves entirely to God and to men. Celibacy is a sign of this new life to the service of which the Church's minister is consecrated; accepted with a joyous heart celibacy radiantly proclaims the Reign of God*" (CCC # 1579).[37]

Here we read "let marriage be had in honor among ALL":

"*Let marriage be had in honor among all, and let the bed be undefiled: for fornicators and adulterers God will judge*" (Heb.13:4; ASV).

In the following passage the Apostle Paul spoke of the doctrines of devils and among those doctrines is a prohibition against marriage:

"*Now the Spirit speaketh expressly, that in the latter times some shall depart from the faith, giving heed to seducing spirits, and doctrines of devils; Speaking lies in hypocrisy; having their conscience seared with a hot iron; Forbidding to marry, and commanding to abstain from meats, which God hath created to be received with thanksgiving of them which believe and know the truth*" (1 Tim. 4:1-3).

Alexander Hislop wrote, "*When Pope Paul V meditated the suppression of the licensed brothels in the 'Holy City,' the Roman Senate petitioned against his carrying his design into effect, on the ground that the existence of such places was the only means of hindering the priests from seducing their wives and daughters!*" [38]

End Notes

1. *Catechism of the Catholic Church*, PART ONE, SECTION TWO, CHAPTER TWO, ARTICLE 3, # 553.

2. Louis A. Barbieri, Jr., "Matthew" in *The Bible Knowledge Commentary; New Testament,* 24.

3. Albert Barnes, *Notes, Explanatoty and Practical on the Gospels; Vol. I* (New York, NY: Jonathan Leavitt, 1833), 32.

4. Sir Robert Anderson, *The Bible or the Church?*, 34-35.

5. *Catechism of the Catholic Church*, PART ONE, SECTION TWO, CHAPTER TWO, ARTICLE 3, # 552.

6. Chrysostom, *Homily 54 on Matthew* ; Accessed July 10, 2020, https://www.newadvent.org/fathers/200154.htm

7. Alfred Edersheim, *The Life and Times of Jesus the Messiah; Part Two* (Grand Rapids, MI: Wm. B. Eerdmans Publishing, 1971), 83-84.

8. Louis A. Barbieri, Jr., "Matthew", The Bible Knowledge Commentary; New Testament, 62.

9. *The Cambridge Bible for Schools and Colleges*; Accessed July 10, 2020, https://biblehub.com/commentaries/cambridge/matthew/18.htm

10. Pope John Paul II, *DOMINUM ET VIVIFICANTEM*, "The Holy Spirit in the Life of the Church and the World," May 18, 1986.

11. Joseph Henry Thayer, *A Greek-English Lexicon of the New Testament* (Grand Rapids, MI: Baker Book House, 1977), 196.

12. Alfred Edersheim, *The Life and Times of Jesus the*

Messiah (Grand Rapids, MI: Wm. M. Eerdmans Publishing 1971) Book 3, Chapter 37, 84.

13. Sir Robert Anderson, *The Silence of God* (Grand Rapids: Kregel Publications, 1978), 75-78.

14. Stanley D. Toussaint, "Acts," in *The Bible Knowledge Commentary; New Testament*, 362-363.

15. Arno C. Gaebelein, *Gaebelein's Annotated Bible*; Accessed July 10, 2020, https://biblehub.com/commentaries/gaebelein/acts/3.htm

16. Norman L. Geisler, "Colossians," in *The Bible Knowledge Commentary; New Testament*, 681.

17. Sir Robert Anderson, *Forgotten Truths* (Grand Rapids,MI: Kregel Publications 1980), 19.

18. *Catholic Dictionary*, "The Vicar of Christ"; Accessed July 10, 2020, https://www.catholicculture.org/culture/library/dictionary/index.cfm?id=37093

19. Sir Robert Anderson, *The Bible or the Church?*, 163-164.

20. Edmond Paris, *The Secret History of the Jesuits* (Chino, CA: Chick Publications, 1975), 9.

21. *Vanity Fair*, "Hitler's Pope," October 1999; Accessed July 10, 2020, https://www.vanityfair.com/style/1999/10/pope-pius-xii-199910)

22. *Atlanta Jewish Times*, "Pope Pius XII Withheld Strong Evidence of the Holocaust"; Accessed July 10, 2020,https://atlantajewishtimes.timesofisrael.com/pope-pius-xii- withheld-strong-evidence-of-the-holocaust/

23. *Ibid.*

24. *Atlanta Jewish Times*, "Pope Pius XII Withheld Strong

Evidence of the Holocaust."

25. *The National Interest*, "Crazy History: What Would Have Happened If Adolf Hitler Died In World War I?"; Accessed July 10, 2020, https://news.yahoo.com/crazy-history-happened-adolf- hitler-030000214.html

26. *Catechism of the Catholic Church*, PART TWO, SECTION TWO, CHAPTER THREE, ARTICLE 6, # 1539.

27. Sir Robert Anderson, *The Bible or the Church?*, 191.

28. *Catechism of the Catholic Church*, PART TWO, SECTION TWO, CHAPTER THREE, ARTICLE 6, # 1536.

29. *The Catholic Dictionary*;Accessed July 10,2020, https://www.catholicculture.org/culture/library/dictionary/index.cfm?id=35745

30. *Catechism of the Catholic Church*, PART TWO, SECTION TWO, CHAPTER TWO, ARTICLE 4, # 1422.

31. *Catechism of the Catholic Church*, PART TWO, SECTION TWO, CHAPTER TWO, ARTICLE 4, # 1424.

32. *Catechism of the Catholic Church*, PART TWO, SECTION TWO, CHAPTER THREE, ARTICLE 6, # 1547.

33. *Catechism of the Catholic Church*, PART TWO, SECTION TWO, CHAPTER THREE, ARTICLE 6, # 1539.

34. Sir Robert Anderson, *Types in Hebrews* (Grand Rapids, MI: Kregel Publications, 1970), 34.

35. Sir Robert Anderson, *The Bible or the Church?*, 191.

36. *Catechism of the Catholic Church*, PART TWO, SECTION TWO, CHAPTER ONE, ARTICLE 3, # 1369.

37. *Catechism of the Catholic Church*, PART TWO, SECTION TWO, CHAPTER THREE, SECTION 6, # 1579.

38. Alexander Hislop, *The Two Babylons*, 220.

Chapter X. The Sacrifice of the Mass

According to Rome the community which makes up the church at Rome participates in the Lord Jesus' own sacrifice by means of the Eucharist:

"The holy Eucharist completes Christian initiation. Those who have been raised to the dignity of the royal priesthood by Baptism and configured more deeply to Christ by Confirmation participate with the whole community in the Lord's own sacrifice by means of the Eucharist" (CCC # 1322).[1]

The Eucharistic Sacrifice

According to Rome the Lord Jesus instituted the Eucharistic sacrifice of his Body and Blood and as a result Christ is consumed:

"At the Last Supper, on the night he was betrayed, our Savior instituted the Eucharistic sacrifice of his Body and Blood. This he did in order to perpetuate the sacrifice of the cross throughout the ages until he should come again, and so to entrust to his beloved Spouse, the Church, a memorial of his death and resurrection: a sacrament of love, a sign of unity, a bond of charity, a Paschal banquet 'in which Christ is consumed, the mind is filled with grace, and a pledge of future glory is given to us.'" (CCC # 1323).[2]

Here is one of the verses from the Lord's Supper, and Rome uses the Lord Jesus' words from the Lord's Supper in order to justify the teaching that Christ is consumed:

"Likewise also the cup after supper, saying, This cup is the new testament in my blood, which is shed for you" (Lk. 22:20).

If these words of the Lord Jesus in regard to the Lord's

Supper are going to be taken literally then we must believe that what is in the "cup," the wine, is the "new testament," or that the wine has actually been changed into the new testament. It is obvious that His words are not to be taken literally. Therefore, the following words of the Savior are not to be taken literally:

"And he took the cup, and gave thanks, and gave it to them, saying, Drink ye all of it; For this is my blood of the new testament, which is shed for many for the remission of sins " (Mt.26:27-28).

Rome takes this verse literally, teaching that what is in the cup, the wine, is actually turned into the blood of Jesus Christ. Rome says the following about the Eucharist and says that Protestants are not always literalists:

"Protestant attacks on the Catholic Church often focus on the Eucharist. This demonstrates that opponents of the Church--mainly Evangelicals and Fundamentalists-- recognize one of Catholicism's core doctrines. What's more, the attacks show that Fundamentalists are not always literalists." [3]

if Rome insists that the Lord Jesus words concerning the Lord's Supper are to be taken literally then perhaps that church can tell us why we should believe that the what is in the cup, the wine, has been changed into the new testament (Lk.22:20). Rome does take a literal approach to the verses in question, saying the following:

"At the heart of the Eucharistic celebration are the bread and wine that, by the words of Christ and the invocation of the Holy Spirit, become Christ's Body and Blood. Faithful to the Lord's command the Church continues to do, in his memory and until his glorious return, what he did on the eve of his Passion: 'He took bread. . . .' He took the cup filled with wine. . . .The signs of bread 'and wine become, in a way surpassing understanding, the Body and Blood of Christ;

they continue also to signify the goodness of creation. Thus in the Offertory we give thanks to the Creator for bread and wine, fruit of the 'work of human hands,' but above all as 'fruit of the earth' and 'of the vine' - gifts of the Creator. The Church sees in the gesture of the king-priest Melchizedek, who 'brought out bread and wine,' a prefiguring of her own offering." (CCC # 1333).'[4]

According to Rome the wine, by Christ's words and the invocation of the Holy Spirit, become Christ's Body and Blood. Rome asserts that when the Lord said, "*Drink ye all of it; For this is my blood of the new testament,*" then at that time He changed the wine in the cup into His blood. However the Lord Jesus' words which immediately follow demonstrates that the wine had not been turned into the Lord's blood:

"*I tell you I shall not drink again of this fruit of the vine until that day when I drink it new with you in my Father's kingdom.*" (Mt.26:29; RSV Catholic Edition).

If the wine had been turned into His blood when the Lord spoke those words then why did He refer to what is in the cup as "the fruit of the vine" instead of His blood? Obviously, the Lord Jesus did not think that the wine had been changed into His blood. Rome's teaching on the Eucharist sacrifice is totally dependent on the idea that the wine is actually turned into the Lord Jesus' blood but if we are to believe the Lord Himself then the wine remained wine and did not turn into His blood.

1 Corinthians 11:25

On the "Catholic Answers" site we read the following:

"*Fundamentalists insist that when Christ says, 'This is my body,' he is speaking figuratively. But this interpretation is precluded by Paul's discussion of the Eucharist in 1 Corinthians 11:23--29 and by the whole tenor of John 6, the chapter where the Eucharist is promised."* [5]

Let us look at the following verse which is found at 1 Corinthians 11:23-29 and see if that verse should be taken literally:

"After the same manner also he took the cup, when he had supped, saying, This cup is the new testament in my blood: this do ye, as oft as ye drink it, in remembrance of me" (1 Cor. 11:25).

If this verse is to be taken literally then we must believe that the wine in the cup was changed into the new testament. That idea is ridiculous so there in no reason to suppose that the Lord Jesus' words which Paul quoted at 1 Corinthians 11:24-25 are to be taken literally. Rome's entire argument about the sacrifice of the Eucharist is totally dependent on the idea that the Lord Jesus' words at 1 Corinthians:24-25 must be taken literally but when it is demonstrated that a literal reading is impossible then Rome is left with no evidence to support her view that the wine actually turned into the blood of the Lord Jesus. Now the verses from John 6 which "Catholic Answers"mentioned will be addressed.

Eating the Flesh of the Son of Man

Rome teaches that if a person does not eat the flesh and drink the blood of the Lord Jesus then he has no life in him:

"The Lord addresses an invitation to us, urging us to receive him in the sacrament of the Eucharist: 'Truly, I say to you, unless you eat the flesh of the Son of man and drink his blood, you have no life in you.'" (CCC # 1384).[6]

Here is the passge upon which Rome bases it case:

"Then Jesus said unto them, Verily, verily, I say unto you, Except ye eat the flesh of the Son of man, and drink his blood, ye have no life in you. Whoso eateth my flesh, and drinketh my blood, hath eternal life; and I will raise him up

at the last day" (Jn.6:53-54).

It is easily understood that when the Lord Jesus used the word "eateth" He was not using it in a literal manner. Instead, He used the word "eateth" at verse 54 in a symbolic sense, and symbolically it means "believe":

" *Whoso eateth my flesh, and drinketh my blood, hath eternal life; and I will raise him up at the last day*" (Jn.6:54).

Here we read that those who eateth His flesh have eternal life and just a few verses earlier He had revealed exactly how a person receives eternal life:

"*Verily, verily, I say unto you, He that believeth on me hath everlasting life.*" (Jn.6:47).

He said he that "believeth" on Him has everlasting life.

The same can be said in regard to His words that those who eateth His flesh "*and I will raise him up at the last day.*" Earlier the Lord Jesus had revealed exactly how one receives the promise to be raised up the last day:

"*And this is the will of him that sent me, that every one which seeth the Son, and believeth on him, may have everlasting life: and I will raise him up at the last day*" (Jn.6:40).

The word "eat" is used both in the Old Testament and New Testament to smbolize believing something:

"*Thy words were found, and I did eat them; and thy word was unto me the joy and rejoicing of mine heart: for I am called by thy name, O LORD God of hosts*" (Jer. 15:16).

"*And I went unto the angel, and said unto him, Give me the little book. And he said unto me, Take it, and eat it up; and it shall make thy belly bitter, but it shall be in thy mouth sweet as honey*" (Rev.10:9).

Since the word "eateth" at John 6:54 is not to be taken in a literal manner then the words "drinketh my blood" are not to be taken literally either. In fact, if the words "eateth my flesh" are to be undersood literally as being a requirement in order to receive eternal life then why did the Lord Jesus say the following about the "flesh" later in the same discourse:

" *It is the spirit that quickeneth; the flesh profiteth nothing: the words that I speak unto you, they are spirit, and they are life*" (Jn.6:63).

If a literal understanding of the words "eateth my flesh" serve as a requirement to receive eternal life then the Lord Jesus would never have said that "*the flesh profiteth nothing.*"

The Death Upon the Cross

It must be understood that the word "blood" as quoted in the previous verses cannot be understood literally. Let us look at this verse:

"*Neither by the blood of goats and calves, but by his own blood he entered in once into the holy place, having obtained eternal redemption for us*" (Heb.9:12).

Since flesh and blood cannot enter into the heavenly kingdom because both are subject to corruption then what is said at Hebrews 9:12 cannot be taken literally:

"*Now this I say, brethren, that flesh and blood cannot inherit the kingdom of God; neither doth corruption inherit incorruption*" (1 Cor.15:50).

In order to understand the meaning of the word "blood" we will examine the events of the Cross. There the Lord Jesus was "made sin for us" (2 Cor.5:21) and the penalty for sins is death: " *For the wages of sin is death*" (Ro.6:23). On the Cross the Lord said, "*My God, my God, why hast thou forsaken me?*" (Mt.27:46).

On the Cross, while the Lord Jesus remained alive physically, He was foresaken or abandoned by God. In other words, because He was made sin for us then those sins separated Him from God:

"Behold, the LORD's hand is not shortened, that it cannot save; neither his ear heavy, that it cannot hear. But your iniquities have separated between you and your God, and your sins have hid his face from you, that he will not hear. For your hands are defiled with blood, and your fingers with iniquity; your lips have spoken lies, your tongue hath muttered perverseness" (Isa.59:1-3).

"Death" does not mean annihilation but instead separation. Physical death is separation of the soul from the body and spiritual death is separation from God who is the only source of spiritual life. So when the Lord was separated from God on the Cross He died spiritually. Sir Robert Anderson wrote, *"We are in the habit of assuming that His work as the Sinbearer began when He was nailed to the cross. But that was the act of the Roman soldiers, whereas this depended on the decree of God. And this was the death He dreaded - not the yielding up of His spirit, for death in that sense was the close of His sufferings, the gate through which He passed to victory. The cup which the Father had given Him to drink was death in its primary and deepest sense, as separation from God. Scripture speaks of it as His 'being made a curse for us.'"* [7]

The Lord's separation from God which resulted in spiritual death is in perfect accord with the death that people experience when they sin:

"But every man is tempted, when he is drawn away of his own lust, and enticed. Then when lust hath conceived, it bringeth forth sin: and sin, when it is finished, bringeth forth death" (Jas.1:14-15).

When a person sins he does not die physically but instead

he is separated from God and experiences spiritual death. The Lord Jesus died for our sins when He became sin for us so the death He experienced was also a spiritual death. In the following passage He said that "it is finished":

"After this, Jesus knowing that all things were now accomplished, that the scripture might be fulfilled, saith, I thirst. Now there was set a vessel full of vinegar: and they filled a spunge with vinegar, and put it upon hyssop, and put it to his mouth. When Jesus therefore had received the vinegar, he said, It is finished: and he bowed his head, and gave up the ghost" (Jn.19:28-30).

Before the Lord Jesus experienced a physical death He knew that "all things were NOW accomplished, that the scripture might be fulfilled...It is finished." So the prophecies which spoke of his sufferings and death were fulfilled before He died physically.

So why would the Lord Jesus use the word "blood" on the eve of the Cross to refer to a spiritual death? Anderson writes, *"justification by blood is to be explained, not by the rites of ancient paganism, but by the teaching of the Divine religion of the Old Testament. For Scripture must be interpreted by Scripture. This caution is needed; for some men speak of the blood in such a way as to provoke the taunt that Christianity is 'a religion of the shambles.' In the symbolism of Scripture, 'blood' means death applied. Therefore it is that we are said to be justified by the blood of Christ. Were it said to be 'by His death,' it would be true of every child of Adam."* [8]

Indeed, if Paul used the word "death" instead of "blood" then people would argue that Paul is teaching that all people will be saved based in the following verse:

"But we see Jesus, who was made a little lower than the angels for the suffering of death, crowned with glory and honour; that he by the grace of God should taste death for

143

every man" (Heb.2:9).

What is meant by "death applied" is best illustrated by the events in Egypt when a lamb was killed for every house, and its blood sprinkled upon the two side posts and upper door post (Exodus 12:13). Then the LORD passed over the door and did not allow the destroyer to come into their houses to smite them (Exodus 12:23). The death of the lambs by itself saved no one and it was not until the "blood" of the lamb was "applied" or sprinkled upon the door posts that the first born in the blood-stained houses were spared a physical death. And in like manner no one is spared from the penalty of a "spiritual" death until the Lord's spiritual death is applied and that does not happen until a person believes the gospel. So when the word "blood" is used in regard to salvation typical language is being employed.

The Priesthood of Melchizdek

The church at Rome asserts that "*The Old Testament predicted that Christ would offer a true sacrifice to God using the elements of bread and wine. In Genesis 14:18, Melchizedek, the king of Salem (that is, Jerusalem) and a priest, offered sacrifice under the form of bread and wine. Psalm 110 predicted Christ would be a priest "after the order of Melchizedek," that is, offering a sacrifice in bread and wine. We must look for some sacrifice other than Calvary, since it was not under the form of bread and wine. The Mass meets that need...Jesus, having shed his blood once for all on the cross, now offers himself to God in a continual, unbloody manner as a holy, living sacrifice on our behalf.*" [9]

Rome says that the OT predicted that Christ would offer a true sacrifice to God using the elements of bread and wine. However, while on the earth He was not a priest:

" *For if he were on EARTH, he should not be a priest, seeing that there are priests that offer gifts according to the law*" (Heb.8:4).

The Lord Jesus' office of High Priest did not begin until He ascended to the right hand of the Father so His priesthood had nothing to do with making sacrifices. Since the Lord Jesus' priesthood is "after the order of Melchizdek" then the priesthood of Melchizdek has nothing to do with making sacrifices. Despite this Rome says that Melchizedek "*offered sacrifice under the form of bread and wine.*" However, the Scriptures will be searched in vain for any evidence that when Melchizdek "brought forth bread and wine" (Gen.14:18) that those elements were sacrifices.

The Unbloody Sacrifices

Rome teaches that "*The Mass is the renewal and perpetuation of the sacrifice of the cross in the sense that it offers [Jesus] anew to God...Through his intercessory ministry in heaven and through the Mass, Jesus continues to offer himself to his Father as a living sacrifice, and he does so in what the Church specifically states is 'an unbloody manner.*'" [10]

The Unbloody Sacrifices of Rome comes stright from the Unbloody Sacrifices practiced in the pagan religions which originated in Babylon. Alexander Hislop writes, "*If baptismal regeneration, the initiating ordinance of Rome, and justification by works, be both Chaldean, the principle embodied in the 'unbloody sacrifice' of the mass is not less so. We have evidence that goes to show the Babylonian origin of the idea of that 'unbloody sacrifice' very distinctly. From Tacitus we learn that no blood was allowed to be offered on the altars of Paphian Venus... the altars of the Paphian goddess were required to be kept pure from blood...The Assyrian Venus, then--that is, the great goddess of Babylon--and the Cyprian Venus were one and the same, and consequently the 'bloodless' altars of the Paphian goddess show the character of the worship peculiar to the Babylonian goddess, from whom she was derived. In this* respect the goddess-queen of Chaldea differed from her son, who was worshipped in her arms. He was, as we have seen, represented as delighting in blood. But she, as the mother of grace and mercy, as the celestial 'Dove,' as 'the hope of the whole world, was averse to blood, and was represented in a benign and gentle character." [11]

"*In the fourth century,*" according to Hislop, "*when the queen of heaven, under the name of Mary, was beginning to be worshipped in the Christian Church, this 'unbloody sacrifice' also was brought in. Epiphanius states that the practice of offering and eating it began among the women of Arabia; and at that time it was well known to have been adopted from the Pagans.*" [12]

Next, let us look at the following verse:

"*And when we burned incense to the queen of heaven, and poured out drink offerings unto her, did we make her cakes to worship her, and pour out drink offerings unto her...*" (Jer.44:19).

Hislop writes that "*we find the women of Judah represented as simply "burning incense, pouring out drink offerings, and offering cakes to the queen of heaven" (Jeremiah 44:19). The cakes were 'the unbloody sacrifice' she required. That 'unbloody sacrifices' her votaries not only offered, but when admitted to the higher mysteries, they partook of, swearing anew fidelity to her.*" [13]

"*The very shape of the unbloody sacrifice of Rome may indicate whence it came.*" says Hislop, "*It is a small thin, round wafer; and on its roundness the Church of Rome lays so much stress... What could have induced the Papacy to insist so much on the 'roundness' of its 'unbloody sacrifice'?...The importance, however, which Rome attaches to the roundness of the wafer, must have a reason; and that reason will be found, if we look at the altars of Egypt. 'The thin, round cake,' says Wilkinson, 'occurs on all altars.'*

Almost every jot or tittle in the Egyptian worship had a symbolical meaning. The round disk, so frequent in the sacred emblems of Egypt, symbolized the 'sun.'...Let the reader peruse the following extract from Hurd, in which he describes the embellishments of the Romish altar, on which the sacrament or consecrated wafer is deposited, and then he will be able to judge: 'A plate of silver, in the form of a SUN, is fixed opposite to the SACRAMENT on the altar; which, with the light of the tapers, makes a most brilliant appearance.' What has that 'brilliant' 'Sun' to do there, on the altar, over against the 'sacrament,' or round wafer? In Egypt, the disk of the Sun was represented in the temples, and the sovereign and his wife and children were represented as adoring it." [14]

"There are letters on the wafer that are worth reading," says Hislop, "*These letters are I. H. S. What mean these mystical letters? To a Christian these letters are represented as signifying, 'Iesus Hominum Salvator,' 'Jesus the Savior of men.' But let a Roman worshipper of Isis (for in the age of the emperors there were innumerable worshippers of Isis in Rome) cast his eyes upon them, and how will he read them? He will read them, of course, according to his own well known system of idolatry: 'Isis, Horus, Seb,' that is, 'The Mother, the Child, and the Father of the gods,'--in other words, 'The Egyptian Trinity.' Can the reader imagine that this double sense is accidental? Surely not.*" [15]

End Notes

1. *Catechism of the Catholic Church*, PART TWO, SECTION TWO, CHAPTER ONE, ARTICLE 3, # 1322.

2. *Catechism of the Catholic Church*, PART TWO, SECTION TWO, CHAPTER ONE, ARTICLE 3, # 1323.

3. *Catholic Answers*, "Christ in the Eucharist"; Accessed July11, 2020, https://www.catholic.com/tract/christ-in-the-eucharist

4. *Catechism of the Catholic Church*, PART TWO, SECTION TWO, CHAPTER ONE, ARTICLE 3, # 1333.

5. *Catholic Answers*, "The Instituion of the Mass"; Accessed July 11,2020, https://www.catholic.com/tract/the-institution-of-the-mass

6. *Catechism of the Catholic Church*, PART TWO, SECTION TWO, CHAPTER ONE, ARTICLE 3, # 1384.

7. Sir Robert Anderson, *Redemption Truths* (Grand Rapids, MI: Kregel Publications, 1980), 115-16.

8. *Ibid.*, 85.

9. *Catholic Answers*, "The Institution of the Mass"; Accessed July 11, 2020, https://www.catholic.com/tract/the-institution-of-the-mass

10. *Ibid.*

11. Alexander Hislop, *The Two Babylons*, 156-157.

12. *Ibid.*, 159.

13. *Ibid.*

14. *Ibid.*, 159-160.

15. *Ibid.*, 164.

Chapter XI. Mary as Portrayed by Rome

No Other Name

The Apostle Peter declared that there is no name under heaven other than the name of Jesus Christ of Nazareth whereby people are saved:

"Be it known unto you all, and to all the people of Israel, that by the name of Jesus Christ of Nazareth, whom ye crucified, whom God raised from the dead, even by him doth this man stand here before you whole. This is the stone which was set at nought of you builders, which is become the head of the corner. Neither is there salvation in any other: for there is none other name under heaven given among men, whereby we must be saved" (Acts 4:10-12).

Despite this Pope Benedict XV taught that Mary and Christ redeemed mankind:

"According to the common teaching of the Doctors, it was God's design that the Blessed Virgin Mary, apparently absent from the public life of Jesus, should assist him when he was dying nailed to the Cross. Mary suffered and as it were, nearly died with her suffering Son; for the salvation of mankind she renounced her mother's rights and, as far as it depended on her, offered her Son to placate divine justice; so we may well say that she with Christ redeemed mankind." [1]

According to Rome both Mary and the Lord Jesus redeemed mankind. However, according to the Scriptures redemption is only accomplished through death (1 Pet. 1:18-19) so "almost dying" redeems no one. Pope Leo XIII says that no one obtains salvation except through Mary:

"O Virgin most holy, none abounds in the knowledge of God except through thee; none, O Mother of God, obtains salvation except through thee, none receives a gift from the

throne of mercy except through thee." **²**

Pope Pius IX taught that it is through Mary that people obtain salvation:

"God has committed to her the treasury of all good things, in order that everyone may know that through her are obtained every hope, every grace, and all salvation. For this is his will, that we obtain everything through Mary." **³**

This teaching directly contradicts Peter's words that there is no name besides the name of Jesus of Nazareth whereby people are saved.

That In All Things Christ Might Have the Preeminence

The Scriptures declare that the Lord Jesus will bruise the head of Satan:

"And I will put enmity Between you and the woman, And between your seed and her Seed; He shall bruise your head, And you shall bruise His heel" (Gen.3:15; NKJV).

In the sign of Leo the Lion it is the Lion who does that and the Lion is the Lion of Judah, the Lord Jesus Christ (Rev.5:5).

Despite this Pope Pius IX taught that it is Mary who crushed the head of Satan:

"All our hope do we repose in the Most Blessed Virgin, in the all-fair and immaculate one who has crushed the most cruel serpent's poisonous head and brought salvation to the world." **⁴**

Alexander Hislop writes, *"The Roman Church maintains that it was not so much the seed of the woman, as the woman herself, that was to bruise the head of the serpent. In defiance of all grammar, she renders the Divine denunciation against the serpent thus: 'She shall bruise thy head, and thou shalt bruise her heel.' The same was held by the ancient*

Babylonians, and symbolically represented in their temples. In the uppermost story of the tower of Babel, or temple of Belus, Diodorus Siculus tells us there stood three images of the great divinities of Babylon; and one of these was of a woman grasping a serpent's head. Among the Greeks the same thing was symbolized; for Diana, whose real character was originally the same as that of the great Babylonian goddess, was represented as bearing in one of her hands a serpent deprived of its head." [5]

Hislop goes on to say, *"Now while the mother derived her glory in the first instance from the divine character attributed to the child in her arms, the mother in the long-run practically eclipsed the son."* [6]

Dave Hunt writes, *"What About Mary? We have identified the woman astride the beast as Vatican City and the false World Church which will eventually be headquartered there. But why a woman on the beast and not a man? Why is this false World Church seen as a woman? Again this criterion, like all of the others in Revelation, fits the Vatican perfectly. The most prominent figure by far in Roman Catholicism is a woman. She overshadows all else, including even God Himself. More prayers are offered to the Catholic Mary and more attention and honor is given to her than to Christ and God combined. There are thousands of shrines to Mary around the world (and hundreds of shrines to other 'saints'), but scarcely more than a handful of minor shrines to Christ himself."* [7]

Despite the fact that the Scriptures declare that Christ must have the preeminence in all things in Rome the preeminence belongs to Mary.

Bowing Down to a Statue of Mary

No one will dispute the fact that today millions of followers of the church at Rome bow down to statues of Mary. Karl Keating attempts to defend this practice in the following way:

"'But God expressly forbids making statues,' say many Fundamentalists. They cite Exodus 20:4: 'Thou shalt not make unto thee any graven image,' and a statue is certainly a 'graven image'--that is, an image made by human hands. When this verse is thrown at them, most Catholics are stumped for a response. If they were more familiar with Exodus, they could skip to chapter 25 and read the account of the ornamenting of the Ark of the Covenant. The Lord commanded the Ark, which held the tablets of the Law, to be topped by--what else?--statues of two cherubim. The statues were to be made of gold, and the wings of the cherubim were to be held over the Ark, as though protecting it. So here we have the Lord, in chapter 20 saying, 'Don't make statues,' according to Fundamentalists, and in chapter 25 the Lord says, 'Make statues.' The key to this apparent contradiction is the purpose behind the making of the statues. In chapter 20 statues used in idol worship were condemned; in chapter 25 statues used for a proper religious purpose were praised. This brings us to statues in Catholic churches. Fundamentalists see us kneel before statues of Mary and the saints and conclude we're worshipping either the statues as such or at least the saints represented by the statues." [8]

The following two verses speak of the commandment under discussion:

"You shall not make for yourself a graven image, or any likeness of anything that is in heaven above, or that is in the earth beneath, or that is in the water under the earth" (Ex.20:4; RSV Catholic Edition).

"You shall make for yourselves no idols and erect no graven image or pillar, and you shall not set up a figured stone in your land, to bow down to them; for I am the Lord your God" (Lev.26:1; RSV Catholic Edition).

God told the people not to make any graven images "for

yourself." So it is not a sin to make a graven image if God commands it but it was forbidden for the people to make a graven image for themselves without any commandment from God. Rome makes graven images of Mary for herself and then bows down to those graven images despite the fact that God forbids those things. When those in the church at Rome bow down to the statue of Mary they are actually bowing down to demons. Paul wrote, "*What am I saying then? That an idol is anything, or what is offered to idols is anything? Rather, that the things which the Gentiles sacrifice they sacrifice to demons and not to God, and I do not want you to have fellowship with demons. You cannot drink the cup of the Lord and the cup of demons; you cannot partake of the Lord's table and of the table of demons*" (1 Cor.10:19-21; NKJV).

The Jesuits and Mary

Ignatius de Loyola founded the religious order called the Society of Jesus (Jesuits) in 1551. J. Huber wrote, "*Loyola had made the Virgin the most important thing in his life. The worship of Mary was the base of his religious devotions and was handed down by him to his Order. This worship developed so much that it was often said, and with good reason, that it was the Jesuits' real religion.*" [9]

Edmond Paris wrote that "*a Novice of this Order, who died in Rome in 1581, was sustained by the Virgin in his fight against the devil's temptations, to strengthen him, she gave him a taste of her Son's blood from time to time and the 'comfort of her breasts'...This worship degenerated into licentious and sensual manifestations, in particular in the hymns dedicted to the Virgin by Father Jacques Pontanus. The poet knew of nothing more beautiful than Mary's breasts, nothing sweeter than her milk and nothing more delightful than her abdomen.*" [10]

Paris continued, writing that "*in his 'Pietas quotidiana erga S. D. Mariam', Father Pemble recommended the following: 'To beat or flagellate ourselves, and offer each blow as a sacrifice to God, through Mary to carve with a knife the holy name of Mary on our chest: to cover ourselves decently at night so as not to offend the chaste gaze of Mary; to tell the Virgin you would be willing to offer her your place in heaven if she didn't have her own; to wish you had never been born or go to hell if Mary had not been born; to never eat an apple, as Mary had been kept from the mistake of tasting it."* [11]

The Goddess Mary

Martin Hudale wrote that "*the Trinity idea of God as a divine unity of Father, Mother, and Child was retained among the Oriental Christians to the days of the rise of Mohammedanism...And this Gnostic Trinity conception is a natural ideal which in the further devolpment of Christianity proved strong enough to inflence the Roman (Catholic) Church in her devotion to Mary, the mother of Christ, whose personality was superadded to the Trinity, and sometimes even permitted to replace the Holy Ghost...In fact, it was common practice for the Catholic peasantry to identify the persons in the Trinity as the Father, Son, and Blessed Virgin Mary.*" [12]

Alexander Hislop wrote, "*It was known already that Popery abroad was bold and unblushing in its blasphemies; that in Lisbon a church was to be seen with these words engraven on its front, 'To the virgin goddess of Loretto, the Italian race, devoted to her DIVINITY, have dedicated this temple.'*" [13]

Hislop continues, asking the following question: "*Is there one, who fears God, and who reads these lines, who would not admit that Paganism alone could ever have inspired such a doctrine as that avowed by the Melchites at the Nicene Council, that the Holy Trinity consisted of 'the Father, the Virgin Mary, and the Messiah their Son?'*" [14]

Hislop concludes his remarks on this subject in the following way:

"What, then, would the reader say of a Church that teaches its children to adore such a Trinity as that contained in the following lines? 'Heart of Jesus, I adore thee; Heart of Mary, I implore thee; Heart of Joseph, pure and just; IN THESE THREE HEARTS I PUT MY TRUST.' If this is not Paganism, what is there that can be called by such a name? Yet this is the Trinity which now the Roman Catholics of Ireland from tender infancy are taught to adore. This is the Trinity which, in the latest books of catechetical instruction is presented as the grand object of devotion to the adherents of the Papacy. The manual that contains this blasphemy comes forth with the express 'Imprimatur' of 'Paulus Cullen,' Popish Archbishop of Dublin. Will any one after this say that the Roman Catholic Church must still be called Christian, because it holds the doctrine of the Trinity? So did the Pagan Babylonians, so did the Egyptians, so do the Hindoos at this hour, in the very same sense in which Rome does. They all admitted A trinity, but did they worship THE Triune Jehovah, the King Eternal, Immortal, and Invisible? And will any one say with such evidence before him, that Rome does so? Away then, with the deadly delusion that Rome is Christian! There might once have been some palliation for entertaining such a supposition; but every day the 'Grand Mystery' is revealing itself more and more in its true character. There is not, and there cannot be, any safety for the souls of men in 'Babylon.' 'Come out of her, my people,' is the loud and express command of God. Those who disobey that command, do it at their peril." [15]

Ecumenism

Ecumenism is defined as the principle or aim of promoting unity among the world's Christian Churches.

John MacArthur wrote, *"March 29, 1994 saw a development that some have touted as the most significant* development in Protestant-Catholic relations since the dawn of the Reformation. A document titled 'Evangelicals and Catholics Together: The Christian Mission in the Third Millennium' was published with a list of more than thirty signatories--including well-known evangelicals Pat Robertson, J. I. Packer, Os Guinness, and Bill Bright. They were joined by leading Catholics such as John Cardinal O'Connor, Bishop Carlos A. Sevilla, and Catholic scholar Peter Kreeft." [16]

"*The statement in effect reverses what the Protestant Reformation advocated regarding sola Scriptura and sola fide,*" says MacArthur. "*The position of the Reformers regarding justification, which was quite biblical, was pronounced as anathema by the Roman Catholic Council of Trent in 1547. Other essential biblical doctrines have been denied by Roman Catholic pronouncements, even recent ones. Unity with Roman Catholicism is not a worthy goal if it means sacrificing the truth.*" [17]

Dave Hunt wrote, "*The key element behind this historic joint declaration is the previously unthinkable admission on the part of leading evangelicals that active participation in the Catholic Church makes one a Christian. If that is indeed the case, then the Reformation was a tragic mistake. The millions who were martyred (during a thousand years before the Reformation and since then to the present time) for rejecting Catholicism as a false gospel have all died in vain. If, however, the Reformers were right, then this new agreement between Catholics and evangelicals could well be the cleverest and deadliest blow struck against the gospel in the entire history of the church.*" [18]

The result of this declaration is that many Protestant leaders have given the church at Rome their stamp of approval and therefore many Protestants will trust the church at Rome come crunch time.

Things to Come

There are many Preterists in the Protestant community, and Corelis Venema says the following about that teaching:

"Preterism, as its name implies (deriving from a Latin root for 'past'), takes the opposite tack of futurism. In this approach, the book of Revelation primarily refers to events that occurred in the past, either in the period prior to the destruction of the Jerusalem temple in AD 70 or in the early Christian centuries leading up to the destruction of the Roman Empire in the fifth century AD...Only in chapters 21 - 22, in the vision of the new heaven and earth, do we find a prophecy of events still lying in the future." [19]

According to this view "Mystery, Babylon the Great" has already come and gone. George Lujack wrote:

"The beginning of Preterism began with Luis de Alcazar, a Jesuit priest, whose purpose in proclaiming the doctrine was to defend the Catholic Church from Christian reformers who rightly began to identify the Roman Catholic Church as Mystery Babylon of Romans 17." [20]

The Preterists teach that Christians are now living in the kingdom and what is coming is a "golden age," which will last at least for a thousand years or perhaps a hundred thousand years. There is also another large segment of Protestants who teach that the world is in process of being set to rights and the actions of Christians matter in carrying us closer to a transformed world. Since the kingdom will be free of racism, war, xenophobia, and injustice then today Christians should take actions that erase those injustices and Christians have the power to accelerate the transformation of the world.

One teaches that the earthly kingdom is now on the earth and the other teaches that Christians are to be anticipating the arrival of the kingdom of Christ on the earth.

Today in many dispensational seminaries "Progressive Dispensationalism" is being taught. H. Wayne House, who was previously a professor at Dallas Theological Seminary, had this to say about Progressive Dispensationalism:

"One of my best students, and a research assistant to me at DTS, had told me in the mid-1990's that he had accepted progressive dispensationalism. My next meeting with him at the Dallas Seminary bookstore just two years ago I discovered that he had embraced amillennialism and covenant theology. When I asked him about this he commented to me that it was an easy move to make from progressive dispensationalism to amillennialism." [21]

"Amillennialism" is defined in the following way:

"According to amillennialism, the present millennial age, which is characterized by suffering, will be followed by the second coming of Christ, the general resurrection, the last judgment, and the new heavens and new earth." [22]

According to "amillennialism" Christians are now living in the kingdom awaiting the second coming of Christ.

However, all three groups overlook the following kingdom, a kingdom which will come upon the whole earth prior to the millennial reign of the Lord Jesus Christ:

"The fourth beast shall be the fourth kingdom upon earth, which shall be diverse from all kingdoms, and shall devour the whole earth, and shall tread it down, and break it in pieces" (Dan.7:23).

The following verse describes the destruction which will come upon one third of those who make up that unholy kingdom:

"A third of mankind was killed by the three plagues of fire, smoke and sulfur that came out of their mouths" (Rev.9:18; NIV).

Surely this prophecy has never been fulfilled in the past so its fulfillment remains in the future.

Andrew Woods addresses that kingdom, writing that "*the next kingdom on the horizon is not the kingdom of God but rather the Antichrist's kingdom. Only after the Antichrist's evil kingdom is personally overthrown by Christ will the Messianic kingdom become an earthly reality. The basic divinely revealed chronology logically teaches that those involved in kingdom building in the present Church Age are not contributing to God's kingdom since God's kingdom can only come after the Antichrist's kingdom has been abolished by God. Rather, they are helping build the next kingdom on the prophetic horizon, which is the Antichrist's kingdom!*" [23]

The teaching that Christians are now living in the kingdom will invariably lead to confusion regarding God's purpose for the Church. This confusion is addressed by Clarence Larkin in the following way:

"*When the church enters into an 'Alliance with the World,' and seeks the help of Parliaments, Congresses, Legislatures, Federations and Reform Societies, largely made up of ungodly men and women, she loses her 'SPIRITUAL POWER' and becomes helpless as a redeeming force. The end of such an 'Alliance' will be a 'Religious Political Regime' that will pave the way for the revelation of Satan's great 'Religious Political Leader' and 'Superman'-- the ANTICHRIST.*" [24]

Those who will be waiting for the appearance of the Lord Jesus will easily be duped into believing that the Antichrist, when he appears, is the Lord Jesus.

Dave Hunt wrote, "*It is easy to imagine Buddhists, Hindus, New Agers, and liberals--as well as both Catholics and Protestants--uniting in a world religion, but the billion Muslims pose a special problem. Mary, however, seems to be the unique one through whom even they could be united into a universal faith. A British Catholic magazine reports that 'a Marian revival is spreading throughout Africa, with alleged apparitions of the Virgin Mary finding a following among Muslims ... ' African Muslims themselves are seeing apparitions of the Virgin Mary and 'are not required to become Christians' to follow her. Our Sunday Visitor pointed out the honor given to Mary in Islam's Koran and the intriguing connection between her and Muhammad's favorite daughter, Fatima. Bishop Fulton J. Sheen wrote an interesting book in which he predicted that Islam would be converted to Christianity 'through a summoning of the Moslems to a veneration of the Mother of God.' He reasoned thus: The Koran ... has many passages concerning the Blessed Virgin. First of all, the Koran believes in her Immaculate Conception and also in her Virgin Birth.... Mary, then, is for the Moslems the true Sayyida, or Lady. The only possible serious rival to her in their creed would be Fatima, the daughter of Mohammed himself. But after the death of Fatima, Mohammed wrote: 'Thou shalt be the most blessed of all the women in Paradise, after Mary."* [25]

End Notes

1. Benedict XV: *ENCYCLICAL INTER SODALICIA*, May 22, 1918.

2. Leo XIII: *ENCYCLICAL ADIUTRICEM POPULI*, September 5, 1895.

3. Pius IX: ENCYCLICAL UBI PRIMUM, February 2, 1849.

4. Pius IX: *INEFFABILIS DEUS*, December 8, 1854.

5. Alexander Hislop, *The Two Babylons*, 75-76.

6. *Ibid.*, 74.

7. Dave Hunt, *A Woman Rides a Beast*, 435.

8. Catholic Answers, Karl Keating, "Statues Aren't Necessarily Idols"; Accessed July 15, 2020, https://www.catholic.com/magazine/online-edition/statues-arent-necessarily-idols.

9. J. Huber, *Les Jesuites* (Paris: Sandoz et Fischbacher, 1875), 98-99.

10. Edmond Paris, *The Secret History of the Jesuits* (Chino, CA: Chick Publications, 1975), 60.

11. *Ibid.*, 61.

12. Marin Hudale, *The Matrix of Mysticism and A Call For a New Reformation* (Xulon Press, 2010), 278-79.

13. Alexander Hislop, *The Two Babylons*, 83.

14. *Ibid.*, 89.

15. *Ibid.*, 89-90.

16. John MacArthur, *Grace to You*, "Evangelicals and

Catholics Together"; From *Master's Seminary Journal*, Volume 6 (6:7-37).

17. *Ibid.*

18. Dave Hunt, *A Woman Rides a Beast*, 6.

19. Cornelis Venema, "Interpreting Revelation"; Accessed July 15, 2020, https://www.ligonier.org/learn/articles/interpreting-revelation/

20. George B. Lujack, *Mysteries of the Scriptures Revealed* (Published in the United States; LuLu Publishers, 2017), 185.

21. H. Wayne House, "Dangers of Progressive Dispensationalism to Pre-Millennial Theology," Pre-Trib. CD 2003, 3.

22. Keith Mathison, "The Millennial Maze"; Accessed July 15, 2020; https://www.ligonier.org/learn/articles/millennial-maze/

23. Andrew M. Woods, *The Coming Kingdom* (Duluth, MN: Grace Gospel Press, 2016),, 363-64.

24. Clarence Larkin, *The Second Coming of Christ* (Glenside,PA: Clarence Larkin Estate, 1918), 51.

25. Dave Hunt, *A Woman Rides a Beast*, 457-58.

Chapter XII. Conclusion

The phrase "*The Battle Lines Are Drawn*" in the introduction of this book means that the main points of conflict between Satan and the people of God have been made clear. Although the final defeat of Satan in this war will not happen until the end of the Thousand Year reign of the Lord Jesus when He will cast Satan into lake of fire and brimstone (Rev.20:10) the Christian is enabled to win many battles against Satan in this war. Paul tells Christians exactly what they are to do in the following verse:

Christians Are Given the Message of Reconciliation

The Apostle Paul told Christians that they are Christ's ambassadors and Christians are to implore unbelievers to be reconciled to God:

"*We are therefore Christ's ambassadors, as though God were making his appeal through us. We implore you on Christ's behalf: Be reconciled to God*" (2 Cor.5:20; NIV).

In the preceding verse Paul declared that God was reconciling the world to Himself in Christ:

"*that God was reconciling the world to himself in Christ*" (2 Cor.5:19; NIV).

We can understand that "reconciliation" is a two way street. God has already provided a reconciliation for the whole world but in order for anyone to enter into that reconcilation he must "be reconciled to God." How does that happen? Christians, the Lord Jesus' ambassadors, have been given the "ministry of reconciliation" to preach the "message of reconciliation":

"*All this is from God, who reconciled us to himself through Christ and gave us the ministry of reconciliation...he has committed to us the message of reconciliation*" (2 Cor.5:18-19; NIV).

In the very next verse Paul speaks of the "message of reconciliation":

"*God made him who had no sin to be sin for us, so that in him we might become the righteousness of God*" (2 Cor.5:21; NIV).

We can understand that all Christians are Christ's ambassadors and are given the task of declaring the message that "God made him who had no sin to be sin for us, so that in him we might become the righteousness of God." That message is the gospel of which Paul speaks of in the following verse:

"*But none of these things move me, neither count I my life dear unto myself, so that I might finish my course with joy, and the ministry, which I have received of the Lord Jesus, to testify the gospel of the grace of God*" (Acts 20:24).

For more on this subject please go to Appendix #7.

The Gospel of the Grace of God

The gospel of the grace of God is found in the following passage:

"*And now apart from law hath the righteousness of God been manifested, testified to by the law and the prophets, and the righteousness of God is through the faith of Jesus Christ to all, and upon all those believing,-- for there is no difference, for all did sin, and are come short of the glory of God -- being declared righteous freely by His grace through the redemption that is in Christ Jesus*" (Ro.3:21-24; YLT).

This translation speaks of the "faith of Jesus Christ" but the correct understanding is the "faithfulness" of Jesus Christ. Christians are not justified by the faith of Jesus Christ but by their own faith. The Greek word translated "faith" also means "faithfulness," [1] meaning that the Lord Jesus is faithful in fulfilling His promises (Heb 10:23). With that in mind let us look at this translation:

"And now apart from law hath the righteousness of God been manifested, testified to by the law and the prophets, and the righteousness of God is through the faithfulness of Jesus Christ to all, and upon all those believing,-- for there is no difference, for all did sin, and are come short of the glory of God -- being declared righteous freely by His grace through the redemption that is in Christ Jesus" (Ro.3:21-24; My Translation).

The Apostle Paul says that now apart from "law" the righteousness of God is revealed or manifested. In Chapter #6 it is shown that the "law" under discussion is the moral law. So Paul revealed a righteousness of God apart from keeping the moral law. And that righteousness comes upon those believing. And those who are believing are "declared righteous freely by His grace through the redemption that is in Christ Jesus."

Paul also says that this righteousness which is apart from law keeping is "testified to by the law and the prophets," meaning that this righteousness apart from law is revealed in the Old Testament. Beginning in the next chapter Paul does speak of believers who lived during Old Testament times receiving the imputed righteousness of God, beginning with Abraham:

"What shall we say then that Abraham our father, as pertaining to the flesh, hath found? For if Abraham were justified by works, he hath whereof to glory; but not before God. For what saith the scripture? Abraham believed God, and it was counted unto him for righteousness. Now to him that worketh is the reward not reckoned of grace, but of debt. But to him that worketh not, but believeth on him that justifieth the ungodly, his faith is counted for righteousness" (Ro.4:1-5).

Then Paul speaks of David who also lived in Old Testament times:

"*Even as David also describeth the blessedness of the man, unto whom God imputeth righteousness without works, Saying, Blessed are they whose iniquities are forgiven, and whose sins are covered. Blessed is the man to whom the Lord will not impute sin*" (Ro.4:6-8).

Now back to Paul's words that believers are "declared righteous freely by His grace through the redemption that is in Christ Jesus" (Ro.3:24).

Redemption

"*But of him are ye in Christ Jesus, who of God is made unto us wisdom, and righteousness, and sanctification, and redemption*" (1 Cor.1:30).

In regard to this translation Anderson writes that "*redemption is not a blessing added to justification and sanctification, as our English versions would suggest. It is an inclusive term, as appears plainly from the apostle's words. But both A.V. and R.V. ignore the 'te kai' in the verse, which ought, of course, to be rendered 'both,' as in verse 24. And no less, of course, the second 'kai' should be translated 'even.' When rightly rendered, the passage reads*:

"*Who of God is made unto us wisdom, and both righteousness and sanctification, even redemption.*" [2]

"*He is 'made unto us wisdom, and both righteousness and sanctification, even redemption'--redemption in its fulness as including all we need,*" says Anderson, "*not only to secure relief from wrath, but to bring us into covenant relationship with God, and to give us access to His presence.*" [3]

When a believer is "redeemed" he is sanctified and that speaks of "access" to God's presence. When a believer is "redeemed" he is declared to be righteous or justified and that speaks of "relief from wrath."

Righteousness or Justification--Relief From Wrath
Justified by Blood

"For the wages of sin is death"(Ro.6:23).

In regard to this verse as it applies to "justified by blood" Sir Robert Anderson says the following:

"The sentence upon sin is death. Man has fallen beneath that sentence he is hopelessly, irretrievably doomed. No law-keeping therefore could bring him righteousness if he is ever to be justified, it must be by the penalty being borne. He must be justified by death, 'justified by blood.' (Rom. vi. 23)" [4]

Next, Anderson explains that God imputes the death of the Lord Jesus to the believer:

"One poem may not constitute a man a poet, but one murder makes a man a murderer, one sin makes a sinner. Nothing but the gallows can expiate a murder; death alone can atone for sin. The law is a standard, so to speak, to which man is subjected - not his acts merely, but himself. If he comes up to it, he is thereby justified, justified by law. If he fails, he is thereby condemned, and law can never justify him; for a law that could justify an offender would be an immoral and corrupt law. The law has pronounced its sentence, and nothing remains but the fulfilment of that sentence. This is the natural state of the sinner under law. But here God reveals himself a Saviour. He gives up His Only-begotten Son to take the place of the condemned sinner, and die in his stead. He now points to that death as satisfying the righteous demand of law against the sinner, and on that ground He justifies him. Not that by virtue of His sovereignty, or by a legal fiction, as we say, He reckons the believer to be righteous while leaving his condition in fact unchanged, but that He justifies him. The believer is 'justified from all things from which he could not be justified by the law of Moses'

(Acts xiii. 39). God imputes the death of Christ to the believer." [5]

Justified by Grace

"For by grace are ye saved through faith; and that not of yourselves: it is the gift of God: Not of works, lest any man should boast" (Eph.2:8-9).

In his commentary on these verses Anderson says the following:

"'By grace are ye saved, through faith.' But error is so insidious and so vital that the Scripture does not stop at a positive statement of the truth, but adds the words, 'and that (salvation) not of yourselves, it is the gift of God; not of works, lest any man should boast.' To speak of earning a gift would be a contradiction in terms; but though a gift can not be earned by works, it may be deserved on that ground. Men's gifts, indeed, are seldom bestowed upon the undeserving. Therefore it is that they so often give ground for boasting. But salvation is not only unearned, but undeserved; it is not only a gift, but a gift by grace." [6]

Indeed, Paul declares in no uncertain terms that "grace" is diametrically opposed to "works":

"For if Abraham were justified by works, he hath whereof to glory; but not before God. 3. For what saith the scripture? Abraham believed God, and it was counted unto him for righteousness. Now to him that worketh is the reward not reckoned of grace, but of debt" (Ro.4:2-4).

If anyone receives a reward based on any "work" then it cannot be said that the reward is according to the principle of "grace."

Anderson also says, *"There are two alternative principles on which alone justification is now theoretically possible. The one is by man's deserving it; the other is through God's unmerited favour. Let a man, from the cradle to the grave, be everything he ought to be, and do everything he ought to do; let him, as our author puts it, love God with all his heart, and his neighbour as himself walking 'purely, humbly, and beneficently while on earth,' and such an one will 'inherit eternal life.' But all such pretensions betoken moral and spiritual ignorance and degradation. All men are sinners; and being sinners they are absolutely dependent upon grace."* [7]

Justified by Faith

In regard to the third and final principle Anderson wrote:

"Grace implies that there is no merit in him who is the object of it, no reason whatever in him why he should be blessed. How then, if the blessing be not arbitrarily limited, if it be really unto all, can a difference be made? how can one be justified and another not? It cannot depend on merit; it cannot depend on effecting a change in one's self; it cannot depend on doing. It must be simply that one accepts and another rejects a righteousness which is perfect independently of the sinner. How accepts? how rejects? accepts by believing, rejects by disbelieving, the testimony of God. 'Unto all and upon all them that believe.' 'It is of faith that it may be by grace": any other ground would be inconsistent with grace. A sinner must be 'justified by faith.'" [8]

Anderson continues on the subject of "faith," writing that believing the "good news" of the Lord Jesus Christ brings life:

"In its first and simplest phase in Scripture, faith is the belief of a record or testimony...Faith then in its simplest character is not trust, nor even faith in a person, but belief of a record...The gospel is not a promise or a covenant, but a message, a proclamation. It is the 'good news of God, concerning His Son Jesus Christ our Lord.' And the belief of

that good news is life" [9]

Anderson sums up his argument in regard to "justification" in the following way:

"The sinner, then, is 'justified by grace' because God can find no reason, no motive, save in His own heart, for blessing him at all. He is 'justified by faith,' because this is the only principle of blessing consistent with grace. And, thirdly, he is 'justified by blood,' because the stern facts of Divine righteousness and human sin make blessing impossible, save on the ground of redemption." [10]

Sanctification--Access to His Presence

Sanctified in Christ Jesus

In the following verse Paul tells believers how they are sanctified:

"To the assembly of God that is in Corinth, to those sanctified in Christ Jesus, called saints, with all those calling upon the name of our Lord Jesus Christ in every place -- both theirs and ours:" (1 Cor.1:2; YLT).

Believers are "sanctified in Christ Jesus." In this verse the Greek word translated "sanctified" means *"to separate from profane things and dedicate to God."* [11]

John Calvin wrote that this sanctification happens when a person is engrafted into the Body of Christ:

"Now the term sanctification denotes separation. This takes place in us when we are regenerated by the Spirit to newness of life, that we may serve God and not the world. For while by nature we are unholy, the Spirit consecrates us to God. As, however, this is effected when we are engrafted into the body of Christ." [12]

In *The Expositor's Bible Commentary* we read the

following about the meaning of the Greek word translated "sanctify" at 1 Corinthians 1:2:

"The word 'sanctify' bears here a somewhat different meaning from that which we commonly attach to it. It means rather that which is set apart or destined to holy uses than that which has been made holy. It is in this meaning the word is used by our Lord when He says, 'For your sakes I sanctify'-or set apart-' Myself.' The Church by its very existence is a body of men and women set apart for a holy use." [13]

In regard to this subject Sir Robert Anderson writes, *"Sanctified in Christ Jesus, called saints," as he had described them in the salutation of the epistle. Sanctification in this sense, therefore, is not a gradual change or a progressive work, nor yet a moral attribute ; it is an act, like justification, accomplished once for all. Just as the guilty sinner passes, immediately when he believes, into a new condition relatively to sin and a righteous God, and becomes thereby and thenceforth righteous; so the defiled sinner gains, as immediately and in the same way, a new standing relatively to sin and a holy God, and becomes thereby and thenceforth holy."* [14]

Sanctified by the Spirit

The sanctification in Christ Jesus is the same sanctification spoken of in the following verse:

"Elect according to the foreknowledge of God the Father, through sanctification of the Spirit, unto obedience and sprinkling of the blood of Jesus Christ. " (1 Pet.1:2).

The "sanctification of the Spirit" is the same "sanctification" spoken of by the Apostle Paul is the following verse:

"Unto the church of God which is at Corinth, to them that are sanctified in Christ Jesus, called to be saints, with all

that in every place call upon the name of Jesus Christ our Lord, both theirs and ours" (1Cor.1:2).

The sanctification "in Christ Jesus" is the same sanctification by the Spirit and both speak of being baptized into the Body of Christ:

"For by one Spirit we were all baptized into one body--whether Jews or Greeks, whether slaves or free--and have all been made to drink into one Spirit." (1 Cor.12:13).

The following verse does speak of the Body being "in Christ":

"So we, being many, are one body in Christ, and individually members of one another" (Ro.12:5).

Sanctified by Blood

Since there is only one spiritual baptism (Eph.4:5) then a believer is sanctified "in Christ Jesus" he is, at the same time baptized or immersed into His death:

"Know ye not, that so many of us as were baptized into Jesus Christ were baptized into his death?" (Ro.6:3).

The believer is baptized into His death and therefore he is "perfected for ever":

"By the which will we are sanctified through the offering of the body of Jesus Christ once for all...For by one offering he hath perfected for ever them that are sanctified" (Heb. 10:10,14).

The ultimate purpose of redemption is to bring a believer into the presence of God. Anderson wrote, "*if God is the Saviour of His people, He has a purpose toward them in salvation. 'I bare you on eagles' wings and brought you to Myself,' was His word to Israel, and such is the great end and aim of the work of Christ to usward. God would have His people near Him. The death of Christ was 'to bring us unto God.' By that blood we are 'made nigh'.*" [15]

The following words of Paul describe how the believer is brought nigh to God:

"*Even when we were dead in sins, hath quickened us together with Christ, (by grace ye are saved). And hath raised us up together, and made us sit together in heavenly places in Christ Jesus*" (Eph.2:5-6).

"*If ye then be risen with Christ, seek those things which are above, where Christ sitteth on the right hand of God. Set your affection on things above, not on things on the earth. For ye are dead, and your life is hid with Christ in God. When Christ, who is our life, shall appear, then shall ye also appear with him in glory*" (Col.3:1-4).

Both passages speak of the believer being "risen with Christ," and since the Lord Jesus sits at the right hand of God then believers have access to God. The second passage says that the Christian's life is "hid with Christ in God" and that Christ is our life. The following sheds light on how that happens.

Made Alive in Union With Christ

Paul wrote, "*...even when we were dead in trespasses, made us alive together (syzoopoieo) with Christ (by grace you have been saved)*" (Eph.2:5).

Here the Greek word *syzoopoieo* is translated "made us alive together."

The Greek word *syzoopoieo* is made up of two words, *zoopoieo* and *syn*.

The word *zoopoieo* means to "*make alive, give life.*" [16]

The word *syn* means "*a primary preposition denoting union; with or together.*" [17]

So when a person is regenerated he is made alive together with Christ or placed in union with Him. The following verse describes that union we have with the Lord Jesus and it also describes the life we enjoy when we are made alive together with Him:

"*And this is the record, that God hath given to us eternal life, and this life is in his Son*" (1 Jn.5:11).

God wants all people to be saved and come to the knowledge of the truth and Satan wants none to be saved. So every time a person is saved by believing the gospel Satan loses a battle over people's souls.

The Grace of God

In the following passage Anderson speaks of the LORD's grace, writing that "*if grace be on the throne, what limits can be set to it? If that sin committed upon Calvary has not shut the door of mercy, all other sins together shall not avail to close it. If God can bless in spite of the death of Christ, who may not be blest? Innocence lost, conscience disobeyed and stifled, covenants and promises despised and forfeited, law trampled under foot, prophets persecuted, and last and unutterably terrible, the Only-begotten slain. And yet there is mercy still! What a gospel that would be!*

"*But 'the gospel of the glory of the blessed God' is something infinitely higher still. It is not that Calvary has failed to quench the love of God to men, but that it is the proof and measure of that love. Not that the death of Christ has failed to shut heaven against the sinner, but that heaven is open to the sinner by virtue of that death. The everlasting doors that lifted up their heads for Him are open for the guiltiest of men, and the blood by which the Lord of glory entered there is their title to approach. The way to heaven is as free as the way to hell. In hell there is an accuser, but in heaven there is no one to condemn. The only being in the universe of God who has a right to judge the sinner is now exalted to be a Saviour. Amid the wonders and terrors of that throne, He is a Saviour, and He is sitting there in grace."* **18**

End Notes

1. Joseph Henry Thayer, *A Greek-English Lexicon of the New Testament*, 514.

2. Sir Robert Anderson, *Misunderstood Texts of the New Testament* (Grand Rapids, MI: Kregel Publications, 1991), 84.

3. *Ibid.*

4. Sir Robert Anderson, *The Gospel and Its Ministry*, 101.

5. *Ibid.*, 164-65.

6. Sir Robert Anderson, *Redemption Truths*, 91-92.

7. Sir Robert Anderson, *The Gospel and Its Ministry*, 100.

8. *Ibid.*, 101-102.

9. *Ibid.*, 39, 42-43.

10. Sir Robert Anderson, *Redemption Truths*, 84-85.

11. Joseph Henry Thayer, *A Greek-English Lexicon on the New Testament*, 6.

12. John Calvin, *John Calvin's Commentaries, Commentary at 1 Corinthians 1:2*; Accessed July 18, 2020, https://biblehub.com/commentaries/calvin/1_corinthians/1.htm)

13. *The Expositor's Bible Commentary*; Accessed July 18, 2020, https://biblehub.com/commentaries/expositors/1_corinthians/1.htm

14. Sir Robert Anderson, *The Gospel and Its Ministry*, 121-122.

15. *Ibid.*, 136.

16. Joseph Henry Thayer, *A Greek - English Lexicon of the New Testament*, 274.

17. *Strong's Definitions*; Accessed July 18, 2020, https://www.blueletterbible.org/lang/lexicon/lexicon.cfm?strongs=G4862&t=KJV

18. Sir Robert Anderson, *The Gospel and Its Ministry*, 17-18.

Appendix #1. In the Beginning

In the beginning when God created the heavens and the earth He created the earth to be inhabited:

"For thus saith the LORD that created the heavens; God himself that formed the earth and made it; he hath established it, he created it not in vain, he formed it to be inhabited: I am the LORD; and there is none else" (Isa. 45:18).

However, some time after He created it to be inhabited it became without form and void and no longer inhabitable:

"In the beginning God created the heaven and the earth. And the earth was without form, and void; and darkness was upon the face of the deep" (Gen.1:1).

Clarence Larkin wrote, "*Some think that when the world was created and fit for habitation Satan was placed in charge of it, and it was then, as Isaiah declares, that Satan said in his heart--'I will ascend into heaven. I will exalt my throne above the 'Stars of God' (other ruling powers) ; I will sit also upon the Mount of the Congretation, in the sides of the North. I will ascend above the clouds ; I will be like The MOST HIGH: and that it was for this presumpous act that the 'Pre-Adamic World' became a chaos, and 'without form and void,' as described in Gen. 1:2. This would justify the claims of Satan that this world belongs to him and that he has the right and power to transfer the 'kingdoms of this world' to Christ, if He would only acknowledge Satan's supremacy. Matt. 4:8,9.*" [1]

Sir Robert Anderson sheds more light on this subject, writing that "*'Ye are of your father the Devil,' was the Lord's scathing reply to the Jews when, in rejecting His teaching, they fell back upon that figment of apostates, the fatherhood of God: 'Ye are of your father the Devil, and the desires of your father it is your will to do. He was a murderer from the beginning, and has not stood in the truth because truth is not in him. When he speaketh the lie, he speaketh of his own, for he is a liar and the father of it.' 'A murderer from the beginning.' The beginning of what? Not of his own existence; for he was created in perfectness and beauty. Nor of the existence of man; for, before the Eden fall, he had already dragged down others in his ruin. His being a murderer connects itself immediately with the truth which he refused, and the lie of which he is the father. These words of our Divine Lord give us a glimpse into a past eternity, when, to the heavenly intelligences, the great mystery of God was first made known - the purpose of the ages, that a Firstborn was to be revealed, and that 'in all things He might have the pre-eminence.' The greatest of those heavenly beings, whom we now know as Satan, claimed that place, and, rebelling against the Divine counsels, he set himself from that hour to thwart them. Therefore it was that he compassed the ruin of our race."* [2]

End Notes

1. Clarence Larkin, *The Spirit World*, 11-12.

2. Sir Robert Anderson, *The Way* (London: James Nisbit & Com., Limited, 1905), 145-146.

Appendix #2. In The Garden

Was it a literal "serpent" or "snake" who beguiled Eve in the garden Eden?:

"*But I fear, lest by any means, as the serpent beguiled Eve through his subtilty, so your minds should be corrupted from the simplicity that is in Christ*" (1 Cor.11:3).

In regard to the Greek word translated "serpent" in this verse we read that "*The Serpent narrated to have deceived Eve (see Gen. as above) was regarded by the later Jews as the devil.*" [1]

In *The Companion Bible* we read that "*The Hebrew word rendered 'serpent' in Gen. 3:1 is Nachash (from the root Nachash, to shine), and means a shining one.*" [2]

That idea fits perfectly with what is said of Satan here:

"*And no marvel; for Satan himself is transformed into an angel of light*" (2 Cor.11:14).

In *The Companion Bible* we read the following:

"*The Nachash, or serpent, who beguiled Eve (2 Cor. 11:3) is not spoken of as 'an angel of light' in v. 14. Have we not, in this, a clear intimation that it was not a snake, but a glorious shining being, apparently an angel, to whom Eve paid such great deference, acknowledging him as one who seemed to possess superior knowledge, and who was evidently a being of a superior (not of an inferior) order?...We cannot conceive Eve as holding converse with a snake, but we can understand her being fascinated by one, apparently 'an angel of light' (i.e. a glorious angel), possessing superior and supernatural knowledge.*" [3]

Following this we read, "*It is wonderful how a snake could ever be supposed to speak without the organs of speech, or that Satan should be supposed able to accomplish so great a miracle (Greater than that wrought by God Himself, who opened the mouth of Balaam's ass). It only shows the power of tradition, which has, from the infancy of each one of us, put before our eyes and written on our minds the picture of a 'snake' and an 'apple' : the former being based on a wrong interpretation, and the latter being a pure invention, about which there is not one word said in Holy Scripture."* [4]

Now let us look at what is said here:

"And the LORD God said unto the serpent, Because thou hast done this, thou art cursed above all cattle, and above every beast of the field; upon thy belly shalt thou go, and dust shalt thou eat all the days of thy life" (Gen.3:14).

In the *Companion Bible* we read the following:

"It is the same with the other Figures used in v. 14, 'On thy belly shalt thou go'. This Figure means infinitely more than the literal belly of flesh and blood; just as the words 'heel' and 'head' do in v. 15. It paints for the eyes of our mind the picture of Satan's ultimate humiliation; for prostration was ever the most eloquent sign of subjection. When it is said 'our belly cleaveth unto the ground' (Ps. 44:25), it denotes such a prolonged prostration and such a depth of submission as could never be conveyed or expressed in literal words.

"So with the other prophecy, 'Dust shalt thou eat'. This is not true to the letter, or to fact, but it is all the more true to truth. It tells of constant, continuous disappointment, failure, and mortification; as when deceitful ways are spoken of as feeding on deceitful food, which is 'sweet to a man, but afterward his mouth shall be filled with gravel' (Prov. 20:17). This does not mean literal 'gravel', but something far more disagreeable. It means disappointment so great that it would gladly be exchanged for the literal 'gravel'. So when Christians are rebuked for biting and devouring 'one another' (Gal. 3:14, 15), something more heart-breaking is

meant than the literal words used in the Figure." **⁵**

Then we read the following:

"The history of Gen. 3 is intended to teach us the fact that Satan's sphere of activities is in the religious sphere, and not the spheres of crime and immorality; that his battlefield is not the sins arising from human depravity, but the unbelief of the human heart. We are not to look for Satan's activities today in the newspaper press, or the police courts; but in the pulpit, and in professors' chairs. Whenever the Word of God is called in question, there we see the trail of 'that old serpent, which is the Devil, and Satan'." **⁶**

End Notes

1. Joseph Henry Thayer, *A Greek-English Lexicon of the New Testament*, 470.

2. The Companion Bible, Appendix #19, 24.

3. *Ibid.*

4. *Ibid.*, 25.

5. *Ibid.*

6. *Ibid.*

Appendix #3. Cain and Abel

"Now Adam knew Eve his wife, and she conceived and bore Cain, and said, 'I have acquired a man from the Lord.' Then she bore again, this time his brother Abel. Now Abel was a keeper of sheep, but Cain was a tiller of the ground. And in the process of time it came to pass that Cain brought an offering of the fruit of the ground to the Lord. Abel also brought of the firstborn of his flock and of their fat. And the Lord respected Abel and his offering, but He did not respect Cain and his offering. And Cain was very angry, and his countenance fell. So the Lord said to Cain, 'Why are you angry? And why has your countenance fallen? If you do well, will you not be accepted? And if you do not do well, sin lies at the door. And its desire is for you, but you should rule over it.'" (Gen.4:1-7; NKJV).

Here we read that Abel brought an acceptable offering unto God and that offering was the firstborn of his flock and of their fat. But Cain did not do what was right because he brought some of the fruits of the soil. That can only mean that previously God had told both men what was an acceptable offering and Cain sinned when he brought an offering different from the one God demanded.

God intended to teach both men that in order to approach Him a death had to be accomplished and the offering was a "type" which represented the Savior's death, a death that provides the means whereby sinful men can approach God. Is there any evidence that both Cain and Abel understood this? In fact, the stars foretold of the death of the Savior.

The first Decan in the sign of Libra is *"CRUX (the Cross)."*

E.W. Bullinger wrote, *"The Hebrew name was 'Adom,' which means 'cutting off,' as in Dan. ix. 26--'After threescore and two weeks shall Messiah be cut off'...In the ancient Egyptian*

Zodiac of Denderah this first Decan of LIBRA is represented as a lion with his tongue hanging out of his mouth, as if in thirst, and a female figure holding a cup out to him. Under his fore feet is the hieroglyphic symbol of running water. What is all this but 'the Lamb of the tribe of Judah' brought down 'into the dust of death,' and saying ' I am poured out like water...my strength is dried up' (Ps. xxii. 13-18): 'I thirst (John xix. 28): 'and in my thirst they gave me vinegar to drink' (Ps. lxix. 21)? The Egyptian name of this Lion, however, points to his ultimate triumph, for it is called 'Sera,' that is 'victory'!" [1]

Alexander Hislop offers the following commentary on what people knew about this death before there was a written revealation from God:

"The patriarchs, and the ancient world in general, were perfectly acquainted with the grand primeval promise of Eden, and they knew right well that the bruising of the heel of the promised seed implied his death, and that the curse could be removed from the world only by the death of the grand Deliverer. If the promise about the bruising of the serpent's head, recorded in Genesis, as made to our first parents, was actually made, and if all mankind were descended from them, then it might be expected that some trace of this promise would be found in all nations. And such is the fact. There is hardly a people or kindred on earth in whose mythology it is not shadowed forth." [2]

End Notes

1. E.W. Bullinger, *The Witness of the Stars*, 48,50.
2. Alexander Hislop, *The Two Babylons*, 59-60.

Appendix #4. Why "Mystery," Babylon the Great?

One of the meanings of the Greek word translated "mystery" is "*a hidden or secret thing, not obvious to the understanding...of the secret rites of the Gentiles.*" [1]

So the title "Mystery, Babylon the Great," is in regard to a secret religious system. In order to understand what was happening in Babylon after the flood it is necessary to have an understanding about the identity of Shem, the son of Adam:

"*In the selfsame day entered Noah, and Shem, and Ham, and Japheth, the sons of Noah, and Noah's wife, and the three wives of his sons with them, into the ark*" (Gen.7:13).

Shem was in the ark during the great flood and after it was over he was blessed by God along with his brothers and Noah:

"*And God blessed Noah and his sons, and said unto them, Be fruitful, and multiply, and replenish the earth*" (Gen.9:1).

So Shem was blessed by God and he also knew the truths which God had revealed to mankind before the flood. Now we will look at what legend says about him, or what is said about him which is not found in the Bible. Alexander Hislop wrote the following:

"*Now when Shem had so powerfully wrought upon the minds of men as to induce them to make a terrible example of the great Apostate, and when that Apostate's dismembered limbs were sent to the chief cities, where no doubt his system had been established, it will be readily perceived that, in these circumstances, if idolatry was to continue--if, above all, it was to take a step in advance, it was indispensable that it should operate in secret. The terror of an execution, inflicted on one so mighty as Nimrod, made it needful that, for some time to come at least, the extreme of caution should be used. In these circumstances, then, began, there can hardly be a doubt, that system of 'Mystery,' which, having Babylon for its centre, has spread over the world. In these Mysteries, under the seal of secrecy and the sanction of an oath, and by means of all the fertile resources of magic, men were gradually led back to all the idolatry that had been publicly suppressed, while new features were added to that idolatry that made it still more blasphemous than before."* [2]

Hislop says that Nimrod, the Apostate, was executed by Shem for idolatry or for teaching things which perverted the great truths revealed by God. So if this false teaching was to continue it must be done in secret. Then Hislop compares that "secret" religious system to Rome, writing the following:

"Was it in a period of patriarchal light that the corrupt system of the Babylonian 'Mysteries' began? It was in a period of still greater light that that unholy and unscriptural system commenced, that has found such rank development in the Church of Rome. It began in the very age of the apostles, when the primitive Church was in its flower, when the glorious fruits of Pentecost were everywhere to be seen, when martyrs were sealing their testimony for the truth with their blood. Even then, when the Gospel shone so brightly, the Spirit of God bore this clear and distinct testimony by Paul: 'THE MYSTERY OF INIQUITY DOTH ALREADY WORK' (2 Thess 2:7). That system of iniquity which then began it was divinely foretold was to issue in a portentous apostacy, that in due time would be awfully 'revealed,' and would continue until it should be destroyed 'by the breath of the Lord's mouth, and consumed by the brightness of His coming.' But at its first introduction into the Church, it came in secretly and by stealth, with 'all DECEIVABLENESS of unrighteousness.' It wrought 'mysteriously' under fair but false pretences, leading men away from the simplicity of the

truth as it is in Jesus. And it did so secretly, for the very same reason that idolatry was secretly introduced in the ancient Mysteries of Babylon; it was not safe, it was not prudent to do otherwise. The zeal of the true Church, though destitute of civil power, would have aroused itself, to put the false system and all its abettors beyond the pale of Christianity, if it had appeared openly and all at once in all its grossness; and this would have arrested its progress. Therefore it was brought in secretly, and by little and little, one corruption being introduced after another, as apostacy proceeded, and the backsliding Church became prepared to tolerate it, till it has reached the gigantic height we now see, when in almost every particular the system of the Papacy is the very antipodes of the system of the primitive Church." [3]

End Notes

1. Joseph Henry Thayer, *A Greek-English Lexicon of the New Testament*, 429.

2. . Alexander Hislop, *The Two Babylons*, 66-67.

3. *Ibid.*, 7-8.

Appendix #5. Evidence For The Assumption of Mary

On the *Catholic Answers* website Tim Staples said the following in his article titled "The Assumption of Mary in History":

"*The doctrine of the Assumption of Mary began with a historical event to which Scripture alludes and that been believed in the Church for 2,000 years. It was passed down in the oral tradition of the Church and developed over the centuries, but it was always believed by the Catholic faithful.*" [1]

Rome overlooks the testimony of Epiphanius, who was an early Church Father (4th century), and he said that "*Mary may have died and been buried, or been killed--as a martyr. Or she remained alive, since nothing is impossible with God and he can do whatever he desires; for her end no one knows.*" [2]

If Staples is correct that the Assumption of Mary was believed for 2,000 years and it was passed down by oral tradition then why was Epiphanius completely in the dark concerning a so-called assumption into heaven of Mary?

End Notes

1. Tim Staples, *Catholic Answers*; Accessed July 23, 2020, https://www.catholic.com/magazine/online-edition/the-assumption-of-mary-in-history

2. Michael O; Carroll, *theotokos: A Theological Encyclopedia of the Blessed Mary* (Eugene, OR: Wipf & Stock Publishers, 1982), 135.

Appendix #6. Whose Top May Reach Unto Heaven

E.W. Bullinger quoted the following verse and his commentary on that verse follows:

"And they said, Go to, let us build us a city and a tower, whose top *may reach* unto heaven" (Gen.11:4).

"The words 'may reach' are in italics. says Bullinger, *"There is nothing in the verse which relatres to the height of the tower. It merely says 'and his top with the heavens, i.e.' with the pictures and the stars, just as we find them in the ancient temples of Denderah and Esneth in Egypt. This tower, with its planisphere and pictures of the signs and constellations, was to be erected like those temples were afterwards...it should have been translated --'a representation of the heavens,' instead of 'a top which reached the heavens.*

"Another important statement is made by Dr. Budge, of the British Museum. He says, 'It must never been forgotten that the Babylonians were a nation of stargazers, and that they kept a body of men to do nothing else but report eclipses, appearances of the moon, sunspots, etc., etc." [1]

End Notes

1. E.W. Bullinger, *The Witness of the Stars*, 10-11.

Appendix #7. Not Counting People's Sins Against Them

"All this is from God, who reconciled us to himself through Christ and gave us the ministry of reconciliation: that God was reconciling the world to himself in Christ, not counting people's sins against them. And he has committed to us the message of reconciliation." (2 Cor.5:18-20; NIV).

There is some confusion regarding what Paul meant in this passage when he said that God is "not counting people's sins against them." What Paul means can be understood when we look at the following words of the Lord Jesus spoken in the synagogue at Nazareth:

"The Spirit of the Lord is upon me, because he hath anointed me to preach the gospel to the poor; he hath sent me to heal the brokenhearted, to preach deliverance to the captives, and recovering of sight to the blind, to set at liberty them that are bruised, To preach the acceptable year of the Lord" (Lk.4:18-19).

The Lord Jesus was quoting from the following passage from the Old Testament:

"The Spirit of the Lord GOD is upon me; because the LORD hath anointed me to preach good tidings unto the meek; he hath sent me to bind up the brokenhearted, to proclaim liberty to the captives, and the opening of the prison to them that are bound; To proclaim the acceptable year of the LORD, and the day of vengeance of our God; to comfort all that mourn" (Isa.61:1-2).

Notice that when the Lord Jesus stopped at "to proclaim the acceptable year of the LORD" and he left out "and the day of vengence of our God."

We are still in the "acceptable year of the LORD," and

during this time God is not imputing trespasses unto unbelievers. The following passage speaks of the time when the trespasses of unbelievers will be imputred to them and this passage is speaking of the day of vengence of the LORD:

"Seeing it is a righteous thing with God to recompense tribulation to them that trouble you; And to you who are troubled rest with us, when the Lord Jesus shall be revealed from heaven with his mighty angels, In flaming fire taking vengeance on them that know not God, and that obey not the gospel of our Lord Jesus Christ: Who shall be punished with everlasting destruction from the presence of the Lord, and from the glory of his power" (2 Thess.1:6-9).

The author encourages edifying Biblical communication. You may contact him at jerryshugart2@yahoo.com

Read other works written by Gerald Shugart, you can purchase his other titles at your local bookstore and online. Most of his works are available in eBook format as well:

Sir Robert Anderson: The Thinking Man's Guide to the Bible

Progressive Dispensationalism and the Missing Throne

Original Sin Debunked

Last Days Fables

www.ingramcontent.com/pod-product-compliance
Lightning Source LLC
Chambersburg PA
CBHW062209080426
42734CB00010B/1855